The Gift
of Prayer

Power for Today's Christian Woman

Jane Schlenvogt

NORTHWESTERN PUBLISHING HOUSE
Milwaukee, Wisconsin

Library of Congress Control Number: 2002114462
Northwestern Publishing House
1250 N. 113th St., Milwaukee, WI 53226-3284
© 2003 Northwestern Publishing House
www.nph.net
Published 2003
Printed in the United States of America
ISBN 0-8100-1505-6

*To my dear friends, who set an example for
me in prayer, who have prayed with and
for me through life's challenges and joys*

Dear Ruth!
Many blessings
to you as you
enjoy Gods gift
of prayer!

Contents

Editor's Preface

For Martin Luther the female perspective was deserving of great admiration. "Earth has nothing more tender," he wrote, "than a woman's heart when it is the abode of piety."

How remarkably true and wise! Women perceive life in a way that is profoundly different from a man's understanding. Sometimes the differences are subtle. At other times a woman's viewpoint stands in bold juxtaposition to a male's view. Subtle or stark, a woman's view on life is inevitably unique because it uses the human heart as its filter.

This book is part of an effort to give voice to the expressions of godly women in every walk and stage of life. The purpose of this book and others like it is to examine the great themes and important struggles that are part of every Christian woman's experience—to help her explore her blessings, examine her faith, inspire her family, endure her suffering, excel in her prayer life, and become fully engaged in the worship of her Savior-God.

In a world gone giddy with the ideology of radical feminism, these books written by women and for women provide a meaningful dialogue bathed in the light of God's eternal Word. May the give and take of these timeless conversations bring glory to God's holy name and a rich harvest of blessings to this book's reader.

Kenneth J. Kremer, editor

Preface

Always read the fine print. A free cell phone in the deal might mean a two-year contract. The free shipping offer may have already expired at the end of last month. The ad for a free cruise might mean *you* pay the airfare to the port city. The word *free* doesn't always mean free. Nothing on this earth is really free, is it?

It is! God gave the gift of his Son, Jesus, to this world—a gift of the highest magnitude. In him we have our life—a free gift. He is our joy and hope for the future—our future life in heaven. All of this is free of charge. And, because of Jesus, the privilege of being able to communicate with our heavenly Father now, while we remain on this dreadful planet, is ours as well. And it too is free—a gift of God's grace.

Two faithful Sunday school teachers were my first examples in prayer: Mrs. Durow and Mrs. Kuntze. They taught my class Bible stories, helped us memorize Bible verses, and led us in prayer. How grateful I am for their patient spiritual training!

My love for prayer grew as my exposure to the Word grew. Catechism classes, personal reading, and my education at Dr. Martin Luther College all enhanced my prayer life, though it has rarely been all that God would have it be. There were hills of growth and valleys of lapses in which I had forgotten prayer's thrilling power. The challenges of ministry, and real life in general, pushed me deeper into God's Word and always took me back to a more active prayer life. The heartaches and joys of life served as reminders of God's love. It was during these times, through this remarkable gift called prayer, that I discovered how faithful God is to his promise to always be with me.

As a young Christian educator, I began listening to the parents of my students speak of their own active prayer lives. I watched them pray together and heard them rejoice over God's answers. My heart was encouraged by their example. When I followed a friend's suggestion to keep a journal of my spiritual life, I began to picture the miracles that can happen through prayer. The practice spread from my home and my heart to my classroom. From there my appreciation and enthusiasm for a life of prayer expanded to include women's Bible study groups and prayer breakfasts. The book that follows seems a natural extension of that ministry. With the gift of prayer we have an opportunity to see firsthand how close God really is to us in our everyday lives. That is what makes this gift of prayer so special. So, go ahead! Unwrap your gift of prayer and watch the blessings begin to flow!

If you, then, though you are evil, know how to give good gifts to your children, how much more will your Father in heaven give good gifts to those who ask him!

(Matthew 7:11)

CHAPTER ONE

Celebrate the Gift

Wedding presents had been arriving in the mail for weeks. As she opened packages and carefully listed each gift and giver, it seemed to my mother that there wasn't anything she and my father would do without as they began their married life together. They had new pans, kitchen utensils, linens, towels, and glassware. There were pitchers, pictures, flatware, and small appliances. Friends and family had thought of everything they could possibly need.

Her 21st birthday fell two days before her wedding. With all the household items surrounding her, it was exciting to think about what romantic gift my father had in mind for her birthday. She didn't expect much; neither of them was a big spender. But maybe he had found the perfect necklace for her to wear down the aisle. Had he chosen a pair of earrings that matched the blue of her eyes?

When the love of her life entered the room, he had a tall, unwrapped box. "Happy Birthday! I hope you like it." Her eyes caught the picture of an ironing board on the side of the box.

When was the last time someone special surprised you with the perfect personal gift? Has it been a while? It's been years, you say? You can't even remember?

As women we know how it can be when someone special thinks he or she has given us the perfect gift. Opening it can be risky; all eyes are on our reaction. We prepare ourselves for disappointment because rarely does someone know us well enough to make a purchase that meets our emotional needs.

Women have certain criteria for evaluating the ideal personal present and unless the gift meets those criteria, we don't really feel loved, right? Who cares if the rules for giving personal gifts are written in invisible ink? Dare I risk putting them in print for what may be the first time ever? Alright, you asked for it:

Rule Number One: Under no circumstances shall it have a cord. Batteries are borderline. Gifts that require a power source raise questions of demanding additional energy on the part of the receiver and are to be avoided.

Rule Number Two: Anything given in the name of love shall not appear on next month's credit card statement, be purchased with cash still carrying the scent of your purse-sized perfume, or arrive with a delivery fee. COD's are out of the question.

Rule Number Three: Scent is a plus, as long as it isn't coming from a liquid fuel source such as the type required by a lawn mower, chain saw, or snow blower. Positive aromas are those that are meant to be applied to warm and pulsing temples and wrists. But scented products intended for soothing aching muscles and joints are especially *un*appreciated.

Rule Number Four: The personal gift should fit the occasion. It is unfair to be baited with a comfortable lawn chair and sunscreen in the middle of December, even if rules one through three were carefully met. This also goes for cross-country skis in July. The rules regarding alternate power sources and undesirable odors are brought into question.

Rule Number Five: The perfect gift must fit. Men may feel safer giving a gift of stylish apparel that tends to be on the small side. This, however, implies he has memories of the past. Too large, and, well, he may foresee you preserving your birthday cake on your hips. Jewelry is an exception.

There is, however, a gift you have received that meets every listed category's expectations, and then some. It comes from our heavenly Father, who knows well every gift-giving rule to satisfy your heart. I'm talking about the gift of prayer.

The ultimate power source

Prayer is a gift—one component of a suite of gifts having an unsurpassed power source. The power source is none other than the grace of a loving heavenly Father. There are no cords, batteries, or alternative energy requirements, just the power of his love. With it he can move mountains, diminish molehills, and help you navigate the potholes and pitfalls of life. Even more important than mountains and molehills, his grace has the power to wash away the sins of everyone who has ever lived. His power is also able to heal the bitter disappointments left behind in sin's wake and to bring the hope of an eternal future to all who trust in his promises.

The gift of prayer comes to us wielding such power. It is yet another blessing from God that we do not deserve. It works in tandem with the gospel—that message of full and free salvation won for us and all people by the blood of the Lamb.

Working together with that kind of power source, prayer surpasses all the high-tech communication resources of our day. You don't plug in, sign on, or dial up. A heavy, heartfelt sigh connects you. A smile of contentment, acknowledging the Creator and Preserver of your body and soul, brings you into immediate contact with God. The aching cry of an anguished heart has his ear. So does a whispered adoration. That is what prayer is.

God does not ask for any contribution of problem-solving energies from the believer. God is the ultimate power source; we draw our energy from him. There may be occasions when we work up a feverish sweat during our anxious pleading. In these cases we are merely exercising our right to bend God's ear. As we plead, our all-wise Lord turns us to the power of his Word to strengthen the muscles of our faith. It pleases God to give us those gifts, such as his Word, which we want and need.

A gift to please the giver

Can we put on prayer as we put on our favorite perfume? Not exactly. But the Bible does use the metaphor of a pleasing aroma to give us a human sense for how our prayers are pleasing to our heavenly Father. In Psalm 141 we read, "Let my prayers rise before you as incense." As the cloud of scent from burning incense rises, our prayers stretch heavenward. (As if our prayers had to *rise* to reach God. But we humans need such visuals on occasion.) Prayers of the righteous are as pleasing in God's ears as the smell of sweet incense. (As if God had a nose. But we humans also need examples of emanations on occasion.)

Jesus died in our place. He sacrificed his life for us, pleasing God in a way we never could (the ultimate in designer fragrances). Our prayers now thrill God because his Son—perfect where we were imperfect—speaks on our behalf. He is the pleasing aroma, the joy of his Father's heart. In Jesus our prayers find their way to the urgent target of the Father's heart. Knowing our prayers please God, because of who Jesus is and what he has done for us, ought to encourage us to pray more often, to douse ourselves in Jesus' holy scent.

A gift for all seasons

Prayer is an all-occasion gift. Every day can be a celebration of life with the Lord as our constant companion in prayer. We can rejoice with him at successes great and small. Our secrets are safe in him; he won't tell a soul. Try taking him out to lunch. Open up a conversation with him at dinner. The rest of the family will chime in following your example. God's gift of prayer is never limited by time, place, or situation. *Now* is always the right time for a few words of prayer. And wherever you are, it is always the right place to quietly speak with the Mentor of your soul.

It will never be necessary to exchange God's gift either. Try it on. Prayer has universal sizing—guaranteed to fit all of God's people. He picks up our signals in a word or two. "Help!" "What should I do?" "What a great day!" (Actually he knew the deep thoughts of our hearts from eternity—we'll talk more about that aspect of prayer in future chapters.)

He enjoys average-length prayers, thanking him for our food and other blessings. He listens carefully to our daily lists of petitions.

The Lord also loves the longer, novel-length prayers that may go on for hours. Such prayers are harder to find. They are most often rendered during troubling circumstances. Funny thing though, even these prayers of epic proportions never seem to wear thin. And though we may ramble, God hangs on every word. In a first attempt at the book-length variety, keep in mind that he doesn't mind if we stumble over words. And God won't correct us in regard to our grammar.

God specializes in sequels. There are continuous prayers that can go on for months or even years. He writes the ending, eventually—the friend you've been praying for since grade school will come to faith in God's time—the son or daughter who has wandered will return as God wills. I've been praying for years, though, about losing a few extra pounds. It hasn't happened yet. (Maybe it has something to do with the chocolate cake I eat for breakfast.)

Ah, prayer, a perfect fit!

An out-of-budget expense

Now, about the price; in our world *you get what you pay for.* The gift of prayer comes at extreme expense, but it was not paid for by us. It was purchased at a very exclusive place called Calvary. Ever hear of it? Christ Jesus paid the bill for our sins with his life. He endured humiliating rejection and suffered beard-pulling and body-piercing of the most painful variety. He suffered emotional and spiritual torture. His own heavenly Father cut ties with him, turning his back on Jesus in utter disgust. The holy and righteous Lord would not, could not, tolerate sin. But Jesus withstood the Lord's divine anger so that his wrath would not consume you and me. He did this so that we could have our own phone lines home—direct lines. He did it so that we could call home to our heavenly Father any time, including evenings and weekends, with no international rates or long distance charges. Talk about competitive rates: prayer is free! It comes in the complete *paradise package,* entirely free—a genuine gift.

However nice it is when someone acquires a gift for us at great cost, do we always appreciate the price? I am aghast at the cost of my sapphire earrings and can only hope I'll wear them at every opportunity. When it comes to the actual value of the gift of prayer, it cost one life, a perfect life. Jesus' sacrifice of love covers money down, high interest rates, and monthly payments of the eternal kind. And still, prayer is a gift that is often neglected and frequently taken for granted. Considering the cost, surely we should all want to make better use of such a priceless gift.

Oh, by the way, for their first Christmas together my dad gave my mom an electric frying pan. He has been practicing his gift-giving ever since.

*L*ord Jesus, how can I begin to tell you what your gift of prayer means to me? You know just what I need—a gift that pleases the heavenly Father in every way, a gift that fits my life perfectly. It is of absolutely no expense to me, though it came at a huge cost to you. Thank you. Remind me to use it often. Amen.

For *what* *I* *want* *to* *do* *I* *do* *not* *do* . . .

(Romans 7:15)

Chapter Two

Excuses, Excuses

I just got a Christmas card in the mail from Gary, a former student of mine. What a lovely family picture: beautiful wife, cute daughter! The letter says he's in medical school now. How wonderful! Feelings of pride and satisfaction washed over me as I read those words. My mind drifted back to the days when Gary was in third grade. I wondered if he still had that dog that always seemed to snack on math papers or the backpack that devoured homework. How could anyone forget dialog that bordered on ritual?

"Did you do your math?"
"I think so."
"Where is your paper?"
"It was in my backpack."
"It *was* in your backpack?"
"I think so."
"Where is your paper now?"
"At home."
"Is the assignment finished?"
"It was."
"What do you mean, it *was?*"
"It was in my backpack."
"Is your paper at home?"
"I think so . . ."

Do they have to stay in for recess at med school?

The best of intentions

I had a boss one summer whose motto was, *If you intend to be on time, you will be.* I have never intended *not* to be on time.

But that doesn't seem to have had any bearing whatsoever on how often I actually get to events (or work) on time. Each week is filled with good intentions. I plan to eat healthy, only one cookie for breakfast. I should not consume numerous cups of coffee a day, but I do, even since my doctor warned me to cut down. I have a collection of lovely gretting cards, since I buy them and rarely send them.

My days are filled with good intentions too. My main intention is to pray. My 1993 journal ended like this: "I want to increase my prayer and (Bible) study time this year, and I know I can do it with the Lord's help." Really a fine focus to begin a New Year! But have I actually seen any growth since then?

My redeemed soul fights with my sinful nature every day about stopping what I am doing in my busy life to pray. My lips can say I want to pray, but my hurried lifestyle (often self-imposed) doesn't always allow time. It's a human thing—part of our sinful nature. In the morning, once my feet hit the floor, if I sit still to pray, I tell myself I've lost momentum. I need to keep moving. I excuse myself, thinking evening is really a better time for me.

Then evening comes. I drag myself and my unfinished paperwork in the door. It's been a long day of teaching, with the occasional meeting after school. Glancing at the clock, I realize I'll be home just long enough to warm some leftovers and maybe get out of my hose and heels. Then I'm off to a workout, then on to a choir rehearsal, which is, in turn, followed by a women's Bible study.

Back home I see the heap of correcting I had dutifully carried home. It's still in the bag.

And there it stays. I need to unwind. A little TV works. But then I wake up an hour later and fumble my way off to bed. Mumbling repentance into my pillow, I promise myself I'll get to those papers and prayers in the morning.

Sensing limits

There are those lovely times when I am able to sit still long enough to touch base with my Lord. Amidst the hustle, we connect. The Scripture soaks in and the prayer flows forth. But then thoughts intrude, however subconsciously: Be careful! That's enough! Don't ask too much! God will answer, *if* I keep the list short.

Foolish thought! God can't be put in such a box. He's not limited to a tight budget of giving. But there I am, acting like the cowardly lion approaching the Great Oz and asking him, "Could I please, please have the courage to speak up?"

Children have no such inhibitions. Our daily afternoon prayer time at school always includes a long list. "Please heal Cody's dad's back. Help Paige's grandma to stop smoking. Help Bethany's grandma's legs to get stronger. Thank you for healing Emily's dad's toes. Help John's mom's side of the family to come to faith. Help us to invite more people to our Mission-to-Kids Sunday. And thank you for my two new cats."

We ought to model the begging and pleading of children. They pray with confidence and without the disabling limitations of an adult's sense of reality. The hearts of little believers are transparent and far more instructive in this regard. There are no boundaries to the prayers of Jesus' youngest disciples. They ask for the moon, even as their heavenly Father has invited them to pray for it.

Abraham prayed fervently for the protection of Sodom (Genesis chapter 18). To his credit, he pursued the Lord with unrelenting persistence, praying the same petition often. But with each repeated request, he trembled, fearful of God's wrath at his boldness.

Why do we sometimes quake like an aspen in the breeze when we pray? Before a powerful and mighty God, our humility drives us. We approach God's throne with that Oz-like attitude. Not that genuine reverence is wrong. It isn't. We have every reason to seek his blessings in all humbleness. We should not forget that we are praying to our *loving* Father, who gave us life and the glory of eternal salvation in Christ Jesus. He is also the Giver of the gift of prayer and wants us to go to him with our prayers so that he can show us, once again, how much he loves us.

I was nine years old when my mother informed our family that *we* were going to have a baby. I had lived with the torment of two older brothers and the sibling rivalry of a sister. The thought of a baby in the house thrilled me to pieces. I could hardly wait. Every night I prayed that the baby would be healthy and that my mother would be okay. Then I always added a tagline to my prayer, spoken with that I-hope-I'm-not-asking-too-much attitude: If it is your will, please, please, pl-e-e-e-a-s-e let it be a girl.

It was God's plan. My sister, Tina, arrived safe and healthy. I reasoned that God wasn't angry after all that I dared to ask for something so boldly and with such persistence.

Satan's deception

Sometimes we allow ourselves to get tangled up in our understandings of what prayer really is. This happens most often when we try to equate prayer with certain communication patterns that exist in our relationships with people. We are deceived into thinking that we ought not waste God's time by repeating ourselves. We don't want to be caught at the Wailing Wall day in and day out with our worries, saying the same thing to God ad nauseum. We rationalize that God must have better things to do than to listen to us whining over and over about all of our petty problems.

Oh, how devious the tempter is! How Satan twists God's promises in our minds! Who else would want us to think God is bothered by the tedious problems of our everyday lives? Who else could want us to imagine that God will be angry if we ask too much? Who else would want us to think that God is irritated by hearing the same prayers from the same sinners day after day?

Prayer lists are helpful tools. (I must be careful, however, because occasionally, in the back of my sinful mind, it becomes more like a department store registry or a shopping list: "Let's see, today I'd like an upgrade on my computer, a new car, and a plane ticket to paradise.") I appreciate having a *hard copy* for keeping needs and praises in mind. The list becomes a wonderful reference when God answers a prayer or even when I'm beginning to wonder if his answer might be a "no."

Sometimes I catch myself thinking that since I've asked God once, now he can look me up on his computer to review the things I've asked for. As if he periodically checks to see how many items on my list have been taken care of. ("Ah, yes, I see that she hasn't yet received the knight in shining armor . . .") When I step back from such notions, I realize that once again I am viewing prayer as God's tool—something that he needs to help him keep track of my needs. But instead it is the blessing he intended for me—a constant reminder of his great love.

Put off 'til tomorrow . . .

I also tend to be a prayer procrastinator. Let's say parents are praying for a godly spouse for their two-week-old infant. I'd say there's plenty of time for that in about 20 years or so. (Even longer if you're talking to a dad about his only daughter.) I, on the other hand, have trouble remembering the things I ought to be praying about today. I tell someone that I will say prayers on his or her behalf, but my promises remain unfulfilled because I forget to put that person on my prayer schedule.

Last year our congregation proposed a cut in our school staff in order to alleviate a hefty lag in the budget. It was suggested that several grades could be combined, thus eliminating one teaching position on staff. The first motion was made in January. At the March meeting the vote was tabled until June. This meant that the poor teacher had to spend another three months fretting over her unsure future. I had tried to encourage this teacher often. "I'm praying for this situation," I had said. And I had . . . as I was talking to her. But each time I sat down at the church voters' meeting and hands were raised as more votes, I repented for being such a weak prayer warrior. I should have explained the situation to the children. *They* would have prayed fiercely about it!

Moans and groans

My personal favorite excuse for failing to make good use of the magnificent resource of prayer is the ever-popular "moans and groans theology for the lazy." It goes something like this: "Surely God can read between the lines of my heavy sighs, brief gasps, and frustrated mumbles. Why, then, should I bother to put everything into words?"

Too often we use the scriptural truth that God knows even the secret things of our hearts to justify our prayer failures. But read the verse carefully. "In the same way, the Spirit helps us in our weakness. We do not know what we ought to pray for, but the Spirit himself intercedes for us with groans that words cannot express" (Romans 8:26). It doesn't say that the Spirit has taken over our prayer lives for us. And it does not indicate that our whole communication with God is released to the Spirit. Instead, God comforts us with the assurance that the Holy Spirit will insert those groans and sighs as needed when we are unsure of what we ought to be praying for.

So what can we tell God that he doesn't already know? Is it possible to surprise the Almighty? I may come close with some of the situations I get myself into, but shock God? I don't think so. Still, the fact that God already knows all things does raise a salient question: If there's nothing we can say that will truly enlighten God, then why pray?

Prayer is a genuine gift that is intended entirely for our welfare. God wants us to ask, even though he already knows. He wants us to pray because our prayer thoughts remind us that he cares and that he is already sending us blessings that we could never fully measure—blessings that we could never stop from continuously flowing (like the air we breathe or the sunshine we enjoy). They remind us he is listening with the deep concern of a loving Father who would (and did) give up his dearest possession for our sakes. They remind us that he has already met every one of our spiritual needs and is eager to provide for our physical and emotional needs as well. The gift of prayer is really *for us,* and we are foolish, indeed, if we fail to make full use of this magnificent resource.

I'm out of excuses, Lord. Help me to live what I believe about prayer. Amen.

The LORD has heard my cry for mercy; the LORD accepts my prayer.

(Psalm 6:9)

CHAPTER THREE

A Package Deal

I should have learned the difference between wants and needs in grade school. Such information is helpful when considering a purchase. Whether something is a want or need affects the way the mind of an adult woman will rationalize a purchase. *I may not need a new bedspread, but since this one is reversible, I'll get double use out of it. This best-selling novel surely is at the library, but if I buy my own copy I can share it with a friend when I am finished. This new dress might be very similar to one I already own but that means I already have shoes to match it.* Are you following my logic?

It seems that we find money for whatever we want. The number of needs already being wrung out of a tight budget does not seem to matter.

Now consider prayer. Is prayer a want or a need? Or is it one of those package deals? "Yes, the pillows come with the sofa." "The belt comes with the pants." A side order of prayer comes with salvation for all believers. Prayer is a package deal.

Part of the package

I like the whole package that comes with being a Christian. Prayer is a free gift of God's love. We *need* the gift of prayer, but it is not the essential element to our salvation; we have that in Jesus. We need prayer as a way of remaining intimately connected with our Savior-God. And because of prayer's great value in keeping us connected to God, we also *want* it. We want to make use of it and exploit it to the fullest measure of its capacity.

19

Prayer has an unlimited warranty, you know. It is guaranteed to last the life of the Christian. God will listen with boundless patience and limitless forgiveness when we talk with him in prayer.

Wanting is an obvious thing for selfish creatures. We want earthly stuff. But not everything we want is really worthwhile. When I was a kid, I wanted the Hungry Hungry Hippos game. I got it. Last week I wanted the plum shoes with the square heels. I bought them. A month ago I wanted a subscription to "Vacation Adventure" magazine. I sent for it. In a culture as affluent as ours we are spoiled because, in terms of stuff, we often get what we want.

But earthly things often disappoint us. The Hungry Hungry Hippos game was not as exciting as they had shown on TV. The plum shoes slipped off my heels and were uncomfortable. Nine months of magazines have piled up and are waiting until summer when I can finally get around to reading them. Our Creator knows about our disappointments. He hates our selfishness. Yet he has commanded us to pray, knowing that through our sometimes selfish and self-centered prayers he will continue to shower blessings upon us in even greater measure.

Prayer has many blessings, though salvation is not specifically one of them. Prayer is not a means of grace. Salvation, in and through Christ Jesus, is part of the total package of God's grace. The message of salvation in Christ, called the gospel, is another part. As is the faith planted by God's Holy Spirit in our hearts through Holy Baptism and sustained through the Word and sacraments. Each part of this wonderful, complete package fills a critical spiritual need in us. Each facet is a necessary element in God's work of mending our broken relationships with him.

An elite communication tool

Prayer is a tool that all of God's people can use to gather in his bounty of blessings. We are motivated to pray with the knowledge that prayer has the power to bring us many benefits. Prayer builds upon the reconciliation with our heavenly Father that Jesus won for us. Prayer is the natural communication that occurs when those in this intimate relationship (God and us) care very much about one another.

Time spent together is a necessary element in building and maintaining a healthy relationship. (The number of minutes spent on my phone with friends makes the telephone company very happy.) Conversely, human relationships easily falter and fade when we don't take time to just *be* together. The same is true of our connectedness with our Father-God. Our relationship dims without regular prayer time. And just as we know when we are losing touch with an earthly friend, we become aware when we have neglected regular communication with God.

Jesus came to earth to share our worries, cares, and to attend to our spiritual, physical, and emotional needs. He knows our heartaches and disappointments. He has himself experienced the pain of rejection, injustice, and the cruelty that humans inflict on one another.

Jesus has also promised that all of our prayers will be heard and answered. Our worries and fears belong at his feet. Through prayer the burden shifts away from us to him. And what better place for our burdens to be shifted? He alone has the real power to do anything meaningful. He alone has the power to attend to our wants and our needs.

I remember the summer of my Miata. (The car has very little to do with the story. That's just how I remember the adventure!) I had driven from Florida to Upper Michigan to visit family and friends and was headed back home to the South. I had one 14-hour day on the road ahead of me and was confident that I would arrive home the next day. But during my two-week vacation I had been oblivious to any news, national or local, and was unaware that a good portion of Georgia was under water from heavy rains. Traffic on I-75 suddenly came to a screeching halt as all travelers were being detoured and sent north. I was completely blindsided. I prayed fervently about what to do next. Almost before I had finished praying, I began seeing hotel signs. Within an hour I was safely in a room just south of Atlanta.

I was singing God's praises! Then I went to dinner and found that the restaurants did not even have drinking water. I was in the heart of the flood zone. And the evening news forecast that the rains would resume at midnight. I had to get out of the state! I showered and dressed. (Escapees should be clean, at least.) And I hurriedly packed my things. Only then did I think again about my gift of prayer. I sat down to pray. My daily devotional read, "Jesus is in Charge of the Storm." I read, "You of little faith, why are you so afraid?" (Matthew 8:26). I cried, repented, and went to bed.

The early morning news showed cities along my "escape route" being evacuated. The streets were under several feet of water. I cried, rejoiced, and went back to bed. "He himself is our peace" (Ephesians 2:14).

Over the years the Lord has taught me to depend on him to have the wisdom I do not possess to solve my problems. He knows that my adventuresome, ready-fire-aim personality has gotten me into plenty of predicaments. Yet he has never failed to bring peace to the self-inflicted chaos of my circumstances. But he doesn't always do things in exactly the same way that I think he will; sometimes he answers my prayers in ways that are even grander than I could have imagined.

The blessings of peace

In so many words, God tells us that he is indeed listening. But how do we know for certain? The evidence is in his actions. God keeps his promises; he does what he has promised to do. And when we consider how God has made good on his Word, we begin with the ultimate sacrifice he made on our behalf. Our heavenly Father did not spare his own Son. What a sacrifice of love! With a love that deep, intense, and selfless, he is most certainly paying attention when we go to him in prayer. He cares about the blood-bought souls of his dear children. There is great peace concealed in his promises. God honors his promises with action.

One area in which children show trust in the promises of God is in their repeated prayers. If God has not seen fit to plant a puppy in the doghouse of their dreams, you will hear about it. Their prayers are sincere and often patiently repeated daily. One school year I found out how many children were secondhand inhalers when the prayer for mom or dad to quit smoking was raised like incense at every prayer time. Later we rejoiced together when several of the children gave praise-reports. Some parents had kicked the habit. God's answers give us reason to repeat prayers—any number of times.

Prayer well-affects the believer's ability to deal with a situation. You may close your eyes at night and pray that the damage to the car will miraculously have disappeared by morning. But alas, the dents are still there in the morning's light. Then as you open your mouth to explain the accident to your husband, a calming feeling comes over you. Maybe it won't be necessary to burst into tears. Why? Because you know that you have the power of the almighty God on your side. He will turn the experience into something useful, something helpful, something that will serve your greater good and the greater good of his people. Prayer brings peace of mind, a welcome change from the anguish and anxiety of the night before.

Peace is the reason Jesus came into this world. (As the clichéd bumper sticker says: *No Jesus, no peace. Know Jesus, know peace.*) He, the Prince of all creation, left his Father's side in heaven to live a humble life in our sin-permeated atmosphere. He did it because God's justice demanded a perfect sacrifice to pay for our sins. A righteous and holy Jesus alone met the job requirements. He fulfilled God's plan for us to be at peace in heart and soul. He freed us from our eternal enslavement to sin, death, and the evil will of Satan. That is a real and lasting peace that no one can take from us.

You've seen the bumper sticker, "Pray for whirled peas." I certainly enjoy my vegetables, but whirled peas ain't hap'nin' in my lifetime. The peace Jesus came to bring to his people is not the kind of world peace most of the unbelieving world is praying for. How misunderstood is God's idea of genuine peace on earth—especially at Christmas! Not that we should-n't be praying for the end of "wars and rumors of wars." The peace Jesus suffered for and guarantees us, however, is spiritual peace between God and us. In this divine peace we are no longer enemies with God; sin no longer enslaves us or dooms us to the everlasting wars that are hell. With peace in our spiritual lives, the everyday struggles of our physical and emotional lives, though hardly inconsequential, are things that we can deal with effectively.

His peace overflows into our other relationships as well. In prayer we have the privilege of being able to approach the Almighty's throne to ask God for healing and restoration where there have been relational rifts and tensions. One of the benefits of prayer is a more stress-free, peaceful you. Burdens are lifted. What a relief!

Bending the knee in prayer

With each successive prayer-visit, we know, through faith, that problems are being unraveled in some way. Even as we speak, a heavenly plan is put into action. As each prayer is spoken, God, in his own way, answers our prayers according to his righteous and wise will. With faith in God's will, we have reason to celebrate the goodness of this rare and precious gift.

With the peace you receive through your communication with the Lord in prayer, you will probably be "coining" a few new prayers. The more you *talk* to God, the more you will *want to talk* to God. The amazing truth is that the desire to pray grows, regardless of the answers you receive. You may not have seen any answers at all. Yet, there is a new and urgent desire to continue to celebrate all of God's gifts. And prayer gives you that opportunity.

Prayer gives everyone an avenue to praise the Lord. It is, in fact, an important part of a Christian's worship life. Many prayers are sung as hymns. Prayer allows Christians to praise their Lord without sending the neighborhood dogs howling. "What a wonderful God you are! Everything you do works out for the best, Lord. Your name brings me peace and joy."

"Come, let us bow down in worship, let us kneel before the LORD our Maker" (Psalm 95:6).

Father, Son, and Holy Spirit, what tremendous blessings you bring into my life through prayer! Fill my heart with longing and desire to visit with you often. Amen.

"This, then, is how you should pray . . ."

(Matthew 6:9)

CHAPTER FOUR

Read the Instructions

I absolutely love the challenge of figuring things out on my own. It's always been that way: "Mom, don't help me, I know how!" "No, don't get out the map, I know where we are."

Assembling something new also falls into this category. I look at the instructions only after the fact. There is not always an explanation for the leftover parts, but what a thrill when the directions show I actually did something right! I even used to collect those extra parts as trophies.

I once bought a bike in a box. A friend and I decided to assemble it together. To pay ten dollars to do such a simple task seemed an outrageous fee!

So confident was I about our do-it-yourself job that my friend's wife and I played a trick on him. When he arrived home from work, there I was, sprawled on their couch. I had an ice pack on my head, my arm in a sling, and an array of Band-Aids everywhere. His wife and I kept a sober face as we told him how I had been riding the bike that he and I had built, and the handlebars had come right off. The shock showed on his face; he had fallen for the joke. We roared in laughter as I removed the bandages to reveal that the injuries were all staged. What fun!

We enjoyed several years of carefree riding together. However, last spring I had this same assemble-it-yourself bicycle overhauled by a professional. He marveled over the fact that the brakes had actually stopped the bike—many times. (How many guardian angels do I have?) And the gears: "Did you know you have 13? It seems you've only been able to use 3."

27

Could biking have been a safer and more enriching experience if the instructions had been followed? I know for sure that I would have gotten more out of my expensive investment if I had used a few more of the gears.

The simple act of praying

Prayer is a simple activity. Any believer can pray successfully without the aid of complicated instructions. It's talking—to God.

Women have a reputation for being very good at talking. But we are often satisfied with superficial conversation. Are we afraid, in the rush of life, to have many deeper relationships? Do we hesitate to let people into our lives beyond the Sunday morning greeting and the casual hello on the street?

I'd venture we would all love to have at least one friend with whom we could share the details—someone who knows and understands us intimately. These kinds of relationships require extra effort. Such friendships deepen with time.

While our relationship with God has been entirely his doing, he does expect some effort on our part now that it has been fully restored. The fact of our salvation gives us a whole new outlook on life. We live to be more like Jesus. If we want to have more than a superficial relationship with God, we need to lay out the parts of prayer, identify them, and be sure we use them all. Understanding every aspect of our gift of prayer can serve to enrich and deepen our prayer experience.

The Lord's Prayer is a great model to follow. It was actually Jesus' diagram of prayer for his disciples. He did not outline each section in detail, drawing neat lines in the sand, pointing out the proper labels. Yet, his model prayer teaches us in the same way that assembly instructions teach us to put together bicycles and other things. The Lord's Prayer can be found in the book of Matthew, chapter 6.

The Lord's Prayer has an introduction, seven basic parts (often called *petitions*, meaning "requests"), and ends with a few words of praise. The first few words of the introduction, called the *address*, remind us to whom we are speaking when we pray.

An intimate hello

Do you recall how the prophets of Baal in the Old Testament clamored all day with the high hopes of arousing an idol (1 Kings chapter 18)? Not necessary with the Lord Almighty. The opening words of the Lord's Prayer are actually for our benefit and show how easy it is for us to communicate with our God. "Our Father in heaven." They serve to identify the person on the other end of our prayer line.

Imagine answering the phone only to have the caller immediately launch into an account of his day. He hardly surfaces for air. Yet, all your attempts fail at identifying the voice. Finally, you interrupt to inform the caller that he has the wrong number. The caller, red-faced, no doubt, is left to redial and repeat everything. What a waste of breath!

Thankfully, we know that the right person always answers our prayer hot line. There is no chance for a wrong connection. He is the head of our spiritual family, our heavenly Father.

Our heavenly Father is the ultimate in everything we hope for in an earthly father, and more. Up in the morning before the rest of the family; at work all day, but always available. (We won't hear the clicking of computer keys in the background as if he's distracted.) What he earns belongs to the whole family. He is a remarkably lovely conversationalist, who always has something especially worthwhile to say, while at the same time being an exquisite listener. Though we may carry cumbersome burdens in our hearts, and we may get quite emotional as we tell him about them, we'll never hear him scold, "Get a grip on yourself" or "Call me back when you've stopped your blubbering." The Lord will listen and love through a flood of tears. And he'll remember every drop. (See Psalm 56.) When we're done pouring out our hearts, he'll dry our tears and start the repairs.

Name above all names

The titles designated for our Lord are indeed precious vessels deserving of places high on our list of preferred verbiage. Our God is identified with names befitting him alone. He is the only one who continually and without fail lives up to those names: the Almighty, heavenly Father, provider, all-sufficient Creator, Savior, Redeemer, Alpha and Omega, Lord above all, Comforter, I AM that I AM, the way, the truth, the life, the gate, living water, Lamb of God. The list goes on and on. These names serve as reminders that he who hears our prayers means everything to us, and we owe our lives to him. "And everyone who calls on the name of the LORD will be saved" (Joel 2:32). So, for our benefit, the first request in Jesus' model prayer is that we would hold his name above all other names by the things we say and do in our lives. We pray, "Hallowed be your name."

Years ago a friend of mine told me about nightmares she was experiencing in which her faith was attacked, and she was frightened by demons. In the dreams she heard herself call on the name of Jesus. And at that point the tormentors always retreated in defeat.

The same name that causes his enemies to retreat in fear is the one that brings incredible and unlimited peace to the hearts of believers. The name of Jesus, uttered by one who trusts in his atoning blood, unwinds knots of anxiety and relaxes waves of doubt. Weights are lifted and we are able to move forward with meaning and purpose.

Using God's name in our prayers is a privilege. Be careful not to store it away high on a shelf of neglected vessels for only occasional use. We can be guilty of dusting off the precious name of Jesus no more than weekly—some of us uttering the name of Jesus in our prayers only in the setting of public worship, chanting it somewhat mindlessly. Handle this name above all names with care, but make daily use of it. Let our Lord's name bring you to new heights of happiness and joy as you bring glory to it in secret sentences spoken to God in prayer.

A far better kingdom

While our own minds and hearts are at peace, our eyes of faith look outward to others in our world. The vision of faith allows us to care about those who are still lost in sin and unbelief. Here we pray that they too may be drawn into this living faith. The prayer "Your kingdom come" verbalizes that desire to share our eternal joy with others.

God has given purpose and meaning to our new lives in Christ. This petition speaks about our role in his kingdom. God uses us to reach others with his gospel. The coming of his kingdom is, in part, through the blessed efforts of women, like us, who turn daily to God for the strength and wisdom to carry out such a tall task.

My dearest friend came to faith as an adult. In faith she has said, "The gospel took my family from death to life. We gained eternal salvation because someone thought it was important, had the courage, and learned the words to share God's great exchange with me. I will be forever grateful to the church and the pastor who taught that man to 'go and tell.' Now it's my turn."

Passing through each day without knowing that Jesus died for all sinners is the ultimate missing piece in the puzzle of life. If there is anything in this life for which we ought not wait, it is to bring the understanding of salvation to those who live in ignorance.

God at the controls

I love to travel. Some of my most peaceful days with Christ have been spent on the road. Travel clears the mind of daily clutter. (Of which many would say I have plenty!) And it provides new horizons and perspectives on life. I love getting behind the wheel of a car and being in control for a dozen hours a day.

Though the activities vary, control is important to all of us. When life gets out of control, we remember what we should have prayed: "Your will be done."

Let go. Women have this mothering instinct, which in more general terms means that we crave to be more or less in control. Somehow we have come to believe that any half-organized day revolves around us and our ability to keep everything going with some semblance of order. As a popular children's book portrays it, the Ladies' Aid chairman shouts orders in desperation from her horizontal position on the way to the hospital. She believes nothing of any consequence will be accomplished in her absence.

Give it up, ladies. Let go. Give God control. (He'll be in charge whether you render control to him or not.) Put your feet up on the hassock of your mind. He will not disappoint you. He will energize you with the deep massage of his Word for your spiritual aching and provide aromatic emollients for your emotional stresses. You'll be ever-so-energized, rising to the occasion on the assignments and expectations that God has outlined just for you. In the "letting go" comes the confidence that God provides for every need.

The great provider

I have an addiction to bread. Today it's foccacia bread. Yesterday it was Texas sausage bread. Last week my niece and I went to the downtown market and bought a loaf of cheese bread for lunch. We ate it all. Every crumb. And by the looks of my thighs, yeast does not cease activity even through digestion. They're not kidding when they say "fast acting" on the package of yeast, but they forgot to add "long lasting." Dare we even think of praying, "Give us this day our daily bread"?

Thankfully, God's bread is anything and everything we need for our bodies. From microwave meatloaf to moo shoo pork to taco salad, our food is a gift from God. Your favorite faded sweatpants, that denim jumper, a yard sale sweater, or last year's Christmas party gown are all gifts from the Lord. Your apartment with the noisy neighbors, the duplex with the cute shutters, or your mansion in the country club are provided for your good by your loving Creator. What about office supplies, kitchen supplies, or school supplies? Gas for our cars, gas for the lawn mower, or fuel for your furnace? They are all part of our daily bread. Have a cappuccino on the Lord. Make mine Irish creme.

I remember one home visit I made as a teacher. It was with a single mom who regretfully explained that her daughter would not be attending our school that year. Her family simply could not afford tuition. The mother had barely finished justifying her decision when the phone rang. The caller offered her a weekly cleaning job that paid (Can you guess?) the exact amount of school tuition, to the dollar.

There's a theory going around about being content. It goes something like this: I'm thankful for the dishes I have to wash because it means I have food to eat. I'm thankful for the dust because it means I have furniture for it to fall on. I'm thankful for the many loads of laundry because it means I have plenty of clothes to choose from. And so on. Try using this theory on your own some day when you feel less than content.

Being thankful for what we have always puts life into its proper perspective.

"Give me neither poverty nor riches, but give me only my daily bread" (Proverbs 30:8).

A new heart

Forgive us, Lord. Forgive us when we are not content with all that you give us. Forgive us when we take for granted our peaceful lives and see another country in turmoil but don't try to help. Forgive us when we don't speak to you all day, but talk about others and put them down. Forgive us when we use your name, but have no thought of you. Forgive us when your Book gathers dust and the romance novels are alphabetically sequenced on the shelf. Forgive us when we tell the truth only if it benefits us and, otherwise, twist the facts for our own gain. Forgive us when we hold grudges. "Forgive us our sins as we forgive those who sin against us."

This petition cuts to the very heart of our Christian faith. What a marvelous God who forgives us when he knows we will still sin! What a wondrous Redeemer who hung on a cross for no sin of his own! What praise he deserves for softening our own hardened hearts in order that we might, in turn, forgive others! There is nothing under the sun worth more to us than forgiveness. And, now, with new hearts, we ask that he would also keep us from sin.

Lead us not into temptation

Disobeying God is our first inclination from the moment our feet hit the floor in the morning. Satan knows the pet sins of every one of us. Beware of his next move should there be any commandment we feel we have mastered. As if the devil himself and our own sinful nature weren't problems enough to deal with, we have the world bombarding us all day long with deceptive ideas. For most of us, the best thing we could do is turn off the TV. That would remove a large share of the temptation from our lives. (There's a switch for that. It's labeled ON/OFF. Pull the plug if you have to.)

I have a friend who, in order to control the television viewing of her two daughters, wired the cord so that the plug was removable. She kept their viewing under lock and key. Too bad moms have to be the keeper of the key. Who is controlling the television-watching obsessions of moms?

Television puts before our eyes every possible temptation known to womankind. Could number 1 be idleness? Then you-know-who comes home to that workshop. He brings along companions such as Discontent and Desire for someone other than your mate and Delusion, making you think less of yourself and your God-given mind, soul, and body. Dare we forget Disrespect for those in authority? Also making a nest are Negative Thoughts, Nasty Language, and Nosy Neighbor. Following right behind are Gossip, Greed, and Get Even. Lord, "Lead us not into temptation" and take away from us every earthly lure that would divert our minds and hearts from our purpose in life, which is to glorify you.

Ours is a sinful world. There will be no utopia until we reach our heavenly home. So, we learn to live with temptation, right?

With a healthy dose of discernment. In this petition we pray for strength to stand against those who would tell us what to believe, how to vote, who our friends ought to be, and those who would lead us to think that modern, intelligent women certainly want to have control of their own bodies, even if it means killing an unborn child. When we hear it over and over from one media to the next, it has it effects. Those of us who believe we can be in continual contact with this so-called "forward thinking" and not be affected are sadly mistaken. It is foolish for us to think we are strong enough to dine on the same earthly diet as the world and yet maintain a healthy faith. True enough, we have a degree of freedom to exercise our will in faith. Paul wrote about it: "Everything is permissible for me." Then he quickly adds, "but not everything is beneficial. 'Everything is permissible for me'—but I will not be mastered by anything" (1 Corinthians 6:12). Pray daily for the strength to stand against all forms of temptation and, in our lives of willing obedience to God, become a source of support and encouragement to others.

Salvation security

Perhaps you've heard this misleading message from the lips of a well-meaning friend, "If you are a Christian, you will have little trouble in life, rarely get sick, and experience next to no conflict." In addition, some think that if you are experiencing trauma, you must "clear your slate" with God, confess some hidden sin, and all will be well. My, how this conflicts with the Word of God! The Bible says just the opposite, "We must go through many hardships to enter the kingdom of God" (Acts 14:22).

Consider Job. Here we have a man who had, in one day, lost 10 children—all of them—and his entire means of income. Job's life was not free from hardship. Yet, he was able to say in faith, "I know that my Redeemer lives, and that in the end he will stand upon the earth" (Job 19:25). Job trusted in a living God who is in complete control of all things. His is a God who exercises control in a way that works things out for the good of all who trust in him.

We pray "deliver us from evil" with the confidence of Job. It is a simple fact of life that we are faced with dangers all around—forces that seek to destroy us, body and soul. The danger might be Satan himself, the evil world surrounding us, or our own nasty thoughts based in our sinful nature. The dangers to our faith are very real—sometimes subtle, other times not.

Not long ago I met a man whose muscular arms had built and maintained a 2,000-acre farm. His broad shoulders had cradled the curly heads of four children. His calloused hands had helped lay the foundation and fortify the walls of a new church and school. As he spoke I became aware of the creases around his eyes and the slight roundness of his shoulders. His personal foundation of faith was challenged by floods and fires, desertion and divorce. Yet no trace of bitterness or regret was evident as he shared with me the joys of his life with Christ. God had not spared this man from the evil things of this world, but he had most graciously delivered this man's soul through a world of pain. For this the man was grateful.

We pray, trusting that God will continue to answer this petition too. God's purpose is to preserve our faith, hold us close to his heart, and keep us as his own. He doesn't want us to become lost to his great promise by despairing over the bad things that happen in our lives.

Glory to our God

How wonderful that we as Christians do not need to live in fear! We have a mighty, powerful God in control of the heavens and earth. We owe our lives and salvation to him. How natural then to end our thoughts with a word of praise: "For the kingdom, the power, and the glory are yours, now and forever." Praise the Lord God; saying "thank you" is a great start: "How wondrous are your ways, O Lord! What a glorious God you are! Jesus, you are so precious to me. How I love you for all you've done for me! Holy Spirit, what mysteries you accomplish and how magnificent is your power to bring faith! What incredible joy and peace are mine because you have control over all earthly powers!"

If we walk daily with the Lord, our foothold of faith will not be lost through the struggles and joys of this life. Even though we may wait for solutions to problems, our cargos of worries and cares are replaced with parcels of peace, light as air.

The Lord's Prayer is a gift from Christ himself, a model for praying women. Its detail helps us see that God cares about every facet of our lives. With our Savior in charge of assembling every aspect of our lives, we can be sure there will be no pieces unaccounted for.

Thank you for giving us this model prayer, given to us through Christ himself. Teach us to pray more fervently, with complete trust in your love and power. Amen.

*F*or great is his love toward us, and the faithfulness of the LORD endures forever.

(Psalm 117:2)

CHAPTER FIVE

A Window of God's Love

Let's talk about windows. Glass windows come in a variety of shapes and sizes and are found on houses, cars, offices (if you are so blessed), and classrooms—the latter more often despised by teachers because they are too suited for gazing.

With the blessing of see-through windows, we have our own view of life. Windows permit us to watch the world go by—foot traffic, rush-hour traffic, air traffic, birds, bees, and biplanes. (Try the view at the Atlanta airport and you'll know all about air traffic!)

The panes in my living room give me a view of the activity in my strategically placed bird feeder. Who would think seeing God's creatures eat could bring such joy?

Some views help us escape our present environment. I simply must have a window over my kitchen sink. Washing dishes is detestable enough without doing it in a box.

Windows let in lovely, therapeutic sunshine. The ideal house has an east-west exposure. Possibilities of fading fabrics or cutting back on the summer cooling bill don't stop me from flinging wide the drapes at sunrise. If I can't have the beach, I'll be happy with a sunny spot on the living room carpet.

Windows also give shoppers an advantage. They satisfy the must-see needs without putting you in debt. There are times when the only way to get a really clear view is to press your nose up against the pane and cup your hands around your eyes. It's childish, but cheap. Try it outside a restaurant. Get a clear view of the pasta and pesto. But, be aware, the view patrons get is not so pleasant.

Though we have ideas about the pearly gates and golden sidewalks of heaven, we won't have a clear view until we get there. Until then God provides us with another view, one that is extremely practical and helpful in this dreary life on earth. The Bible is a window into God's own heart. Seeing our God through his Word, we can know his work, his plans, his wisdom, his love, and his will for his people. And knowing the heart of our God teaches us how to respond and interact with him in prayer.

Here's an example: We see clearly from Genesis that God created this world and all the lovely scenes we enjoy. God's window, the Word, says, "In the beginning God created the heavens and the earth" (Genesis 1:1). It is easy to see God's hand in springtime—purple crocus peeping through the snow, yellow daffodils against the white siding, the first finches at your feeder. Knowing that God is the Creator of all things leads us to thank and praise him for his wisdom and love in giving the gift of this world to us. In prayer we celebrate the joy and the appreciation we have for his created world.

God's Word is also a wonderful window for seeing that his hand still guides the people he created. "'For I know the plans I have for you,' declares the LORD, 'plans to prosper you and not to harm you, plans to give you hope and a future'" (Jeremiah 29:11). Knowing God has only good in mind for us helps us enjoy the view from the pinnacles of life as well as the darkened valleys we must travel. Our praise is all he asks for his services.

God's Word also works as the ever-humbling two-way glass. We see into God's heart through Scripture, but the powerful Word of God is also capable of showing us our own hearts. All those pet sins we insist we have put behind us are brought to light. We see ourselves in the mirror of God's law. Not a good sight! "You shall not steal." (You keep your thumb on the expired date of the coupon as you hand it over, hoping the clerk does not check it.) "You shall not covet." (I continually drool over the new neighborhoods I pass, wondering who can afford to live there and wishing all the time that I did.)

God sees through the two-way glass too. His eyes are on us as we fudge our taxes, slander a sibling, or sneak an extra newspaper from the vending box. There is nothing we can hide from him. The question is: how can we survive even one day with the righteous judge of heaven and earth knowing everything we've said and done?

Thankfully, his forgiving eyes of love are also on us day and night. He refuses to zap us because our sins have already been dealt with in the life and death of his own dear Son. Joy of joys! What shines through Scripture most clearly is the brilliant light of that forgiveness. We have salvation in Jesus. "Because of his great love for us, God, who is rich in mercy, made us alive with Christ even when we were dead in transgressions—it is by grace you have been saved" (Ephesians 2:4).

But let's go back to the two-way glass because there is another aspect to this reflecting glass that still needs to be examined. Our view of God's law through the window of his Word serves to show us our mistakes, our sinful blunders. But the focus of God's law itself is to bring us to repentance. His watchful eyes, peering through the windows of heaven, keep us in his grace. When he views us through the law, it is for the purpose of correction. "Blessed is the man [woman] you discipline, O LORD, the man [woman] you teach from your law . . . When I said, 'My foot is slipping,' your love, O LORD, supported me" (Psalm 94:12,18).

Why such an emphasis on correction? Covered in the blood of Jesus, we know God sees us as perfect. We are sure of heaven. But if our hearts are turned to sin, how can we expect a holy God to hear our prayers? "Therefore confess your sins to each other and pray for each other so that you may be healed. The prayer of a righteous man [woman] is powerful and effective" (James 5:16).

Let the mirror of the law show you your sin so that you may repent. Let the light of the gospel comfort your spirit and give you a peace that transcends the things of this life. And let your prayers be "powerful and effective" by God's grace to help you deal with the obstacles and barriers of this life.

According to God's will

Are there some prayers that are more effective than others?

Prayers that are prayed according to God's will are guaranteed his answers. "This is the confidence we have in approaching God: that if we ask anything according to his will, he hears us. And if we know that he hears us—whatever we ask—we know that we have what we asked of him" (1 John 5:14,15).

How can we know the will of the Lord? Look into the window of the Word to learn what God wills, and then pray accordingly. God will never fail to hear and answer prayers for an increase in love, joy, peace, patience, kindness, goodness, gentleness, faithfulness, and self-control. Did you recognize these as the fruits of the Spirit? (See Galatians chapter 5.) It is God's will that all of his people would share in these gifts of the Holy Spirit.

The idea here is to pray those prayers to which God cannot say no.

For years I prayed vague prayers such as: "Let me be a good teacher." "Help me to be a better friend." "Let me get along with everyone." I noticed a dramatic difference in life and relationships when God led me to pray, "Lord, let me love your people better."

God will not say no to an increase in love. He commands us to love. First, we love him. ("Love the Lord your God with all your heart and with all your soul and with all your mind" [Matthew 22:37].) Then we are free to love others. ("Love your neighbor as yourself" [Matthew 22:39].) When God increased the love in my heart for others, I was, in turn, a better teacher, friend, and church leader.

Now the hard part: "Love your enemies and pray for those who persecute you" (Matthew 5:44). Loving some people is like handing over your life savings to a gambler. You don't believe they deserve it. It will be a total waste. You'll never see your money again.

A few weeks ago in a crowded church I found that the ushers had seated me next to a scowler. You know the type—they don't look you in the eye, rarely smile, and leave you wondering what you did. I felt trapped. I repented of not loving all God's people the same. I prayed, "God give me the strength and courage to show love to her." After the service I cheerfully greeted her and launched into the joys of spring in Wisconsin. She turned to me with a smile and responded with stories of spring gardening. Thank you, Lord, for an increase of love.

Amplifying the joy

Ministry became so much more fulfilling as I grew in love for God's people. I started to see how often people lacked true joy. I began to pray that God would add to my mission. Along with teaching children and leading adults in song, I wanted him to use me to share joy. What a responsibility! And not an easy task, since I wasn't blessed with much joy before 10:00 A.M. And since my other down time of the day is between 4:00 and 6:00 P.M., it was a challenge to be cheerful during after-school hours too. For years I prayed and practiced. Then eventually joy began to overflow in my life. I knew things had changed when, one week into a new school year, another teacher commented, "I like having you around because you smile all the time." Thank you, Lord, for joy.

God promises joy to his people in spite of rotten circumstances. A favorite Scripture text where God promises joy is in Habakkuk.

> Though the fig tree does not bud and there are no grapes on the vines, though the olive crop fails and the fields produce no food, though there are no sheep in the pen and no cattle in the stalls, yet I will rejoice in the LORD, I will be joyful in God my Savior. The Sovereign LORD is my strength; he makes my feet like the feet of a deer, he enables me to go on the heights. (Habakkuk 3:17-19)

Let God bring you to the heights today. Pray for joy . . . then share it.

We can know the heart of God through the window of his Word. We see his wisdom and will. We repent and rejoice in the Savior. Then we pick a fruit and pray. All the fruits of the spirit are available for the asking: love, joy, peace, patience, kindness, goodness, faithfulness, gentleness, and self-control. Just "ask and it will be given to you" (Matthew 7:7). Then sit back and enjoy the view as God adds seconds and thirds of *fruit salad* to the plate of your life.

T hank you, Lord, for the view of your heart that you give me through your Word. Improve my prayer life as I seek to know your will. Then help me live according to your will, with joy and a sense of purpose. Amen.

O LORD, our Lord, how majestic is your name in all the earth!
(Psalm 8:1)

CHAPTER SIX

A Recyclable Gift

The short list of my recyclable collection includes 16 peanut butter jars, 57 yogurt containers in a variety of sizes, 33 corks, and 19 ice cream buckets. I seal blackberry jam in the jars. Yogurt containers are just right for leftovers. Birdseed, laundry detergent, potting soil, and even rice go into the buckets. I haven't even mentioned the craft supplies. My friends give me a hard time about being a pack rat. But how I love those Thursday night calls from fellow teachers in need of supplies for Friday's art project!

I don't think there's a cure for pack-ratitis. Being a saver can be a pain. Storage becomes an issue. My Florida landlord was ready to build me a storage shed. Then I moved. Moving is the only way to purge. Even then it's hard to part with some stuff. It's all so usable. You can't put a price on eight years of *Good Housekeeping* back issues. I've gotten pretty efficient at rescuing great recipes from the jaws of student scissors.

There are times when even this pack rat becomes the borrower instead of the borrowee. I need something I simply cannot get enough of, yet always seem to run out of: words. Just the right words. Prayer words. Words that say what my spirit is feeling, but is unable to express—a sentence I would speak *if* I had thought of it—a request I would have made *if* I had known what I needed—or *if* I had been aware that someone else was in need.

The word warehouse

Our God is a keeper of words—not just any words but mean-ingful words, useful words, powerful words. He doesn't have a storage problem; his words (the Bible) can fit in a space about the size of a compact purse or pocket size storage container.

Some remarkable things happen when his words come in contact with human hearts. He is able to plant them deep in the souls of men and women and children, like seed. Moreover, these words remove stains on the soul like my detergent cleans laundry. They grow faith, flower, and bear fruit. The sacred words of the Lord feed the spiritually hungry around the world, like many grains of rice.

And when he's done using his words to tell us about himself and his plan for our lives, God gives away words for us to use where we are lacking. He provides exact words to verbalize our sighs, our expressions of confusion or doubt, our exasperation. He puts syllables together to provide praises and exaltations. All the words we need are right at our fingertips, written down just for us.

God's Word has many verses that echo in our thoughts and prayers. The Psalms contain prayers written from God's heart through human minds. When God's Word is quoted in another source, I often am driven to turn to the context. I need to see for myself whether God could know me so well as to make every word fit my life so perfectly. How my heart warms and my spirit soars to find that God knows my needs so specifically!

Using the very words of God to pray ensures that we are praying his will. After all, God has inspired these words. Of course that assumes we have not dared to take his words out of context. (You may have heard of this example of taking Scripture out of context: "Then Judas went away and hanged himself . . . Go and do likewise." It's a given that we use common sense.)

A prayer plan

Scripture has words of praise perfect for the beginning of my day: "The LORD lives! Praise be to my Rock! Exalted be God my Savior!" (Psalm 18:46); or "I love you, O LORD, my strength" (Psalm 18:1).

But it was not exactly praise on my lips one March. I'd heard all the stories and read all the T-shirts about what it was like to turn 40. Of course I had hoped to be the exception. I'd had a particularly hectic time the few weeks before my birthday. I remember realizing I hadn't seen my bed before midnight in at least two weeks. Among other things I had been out of town with family, lining up things for the spring musical, finishing paperwork, and planning all that endless homework teachers are known for. A friend and her children came to town to celebrate my birthday with me. As they slept in, I remember stumbling from my bed, aching from head to toe, and heading straight to the sink to take two ibuprofen. Getting older makes me rejoice each morning that I am still alive. But when I rejoice even more that *God* is alive, I start feeling better inside and out.

Before moving headlong into a day, I pray for focus and faithfulness: "Lead me, O LORD, in your righteousness because of my enemies—make straight your way before me" (Psalm 5:8). Whatever neighborhood dog, cranky coworker, or overdue project lies before you, it's important to ask God to be there with you to keep you from sin and to bless your work. Some days I'm thankful for a straight path to the copy machine.

How about starting a morning family time? Join the children in a chorus of Psalm 17: "Keep me as the apple of your eye; hide me in the shadow of your wings" (verse 8). How about an evening family prayer of praise? Psalm 40:5 works well. Feel free to adjust the pronouns as needed. "Many, O LORD my (our) God, are the wonders you have done. The things you planned for us no one can recount to you; were I (we) to speak and tell of them, they would be too many to declare." Why not continue the prayer by asking his blessing on specific events happening that day? Pray also for preparedness to deal with unplanned events.

Without even a pet to entertain me, I must confess that the telephone has become my outlet. I knew I had an addiction when my phone bill reported 742 minutes in February . . . to

49

one friend! And that's only my end of the charges. (At least it wasn't international!) If only I would spend 742 minutes a month in prayer, some major mountains could be moved.

Our speech is certainly modified when we remember God is listening. At one time friends of mine kept their lovebird near the phone. They knew they had another set of ears in the house when the bird mimicked in its high-pitched voice, "Hello? Uhuh . . . uhuh . . . ohh . . . uhuh . . . really?" A good prayer verse to post near any form of communication might be, "May the words of my mouth and the meditation of my heart be pleasing in your sight, O LORD, my Rock and my Redeemer" (Psalm 19:14).

Above the water tap on my refrigerator I keep this prayer, "As the deer pants for streams of water, so my soul pants for you, O God. My soul thirsts for God, for the living God" (Psalm 42:1,2). And then I add my own thought: *Let us daily thirst for your Word.*

Praying can make you feel like you're the one doing all the talking. A music director I know practices breath control on the telephone. She talks as long as she can on one breath. She claims to be so good, no one can get a word in edgewise. God lets us talk; he will not cut us off. There are prayers in Scripture that remind us that God is always listening: "Give ear to my words, O LORD, consider my sighing. Listen to my cry for help, my King and my God, for to you I pray" (Psalm 5:1,2).

If you're like me, about ten steps into your day you've already blundered. I'm already repenting before I'm out the door, usually because I'm late, late, late. I think David had bad days too since this is the very first verse of one of his psalms, "O LORD, do not rebuke me in your anger or discipline me in your wrath" (Psalm 38:1).

You might continue with a prayer for deliverance from a personal sin or from the evil caused by our sinful world. "Arise, O LORD! Deliver me, O my God!" (Psalm 3:7). "Answer me when I call to you, O my righteous God. Give me relief from my distress; be merciful to me and hear my prayer" (Psalm 4:1). Keep in mind, you still may face the consequences of your blunders!

In order to face the consequences you will no doubt need a prayer for strength: "With your help I can advance against a troop; with my God I can scale a wall" (Psalm 18:29). (Sorry, I could not find a verse about getting past the boss without him seeing you sneaking in late again. Believe me, I searched.)

We might question the need for a prayer asking for justice. At what time would you call divine consequences down on someone? Calling down God's discipline on another person can be a loving thing to do. David prayed, "Strike them with terror, O LORD; let the nations know they are but men" (Psalm 9:20).

I first came across this prayer on a day when I had literally taken refuge. It was supposed to have been the first day of school, but our school's students and faculty had instead gathered at the parsonage for protection from a storm. It was August of 1992 and Hurricane Andrew had struck the east coast of Florida overnight. News reports had shown the unbelievable destruction Andrew had already caused. Knowing God has a purpose in all things, and the greatest good for all, I prayed David's words from Psalm 9. And "strike them with terror" he had. God's purpose was served. Through the peoples' terror, many remembered and were drawn to the strength of their childhood faith. Others sought out a local church for the first time. Through newspapers and television people shared their new-found faith.

Have you ever noticed that in most prayer lists—whether made by an individual, a family, in a classroom, or in a Sunday service—the easiest thing to pray about seems to be sickness? What a wonder that we're often neglectful of the spiritual condition! Earthly destruction as well as physical sickness often lead people to the Source of Strength.

It's important for me to keep supplies on hand for potential sick days, specifically, one or two cans of chicken soup. With stars. Being sick by yourself is worse than the sore throat, muscle aches, headaches, or whatever ails you. There are medications for those things. There is no prescription for loneliness, except the Word. "Turn to me and be gracious to me, for I am lonely and afflicted" (Psalm 25:16). What a combination: lonely and afflicted! God has the answer to everything. Take two psalms and call him in the morning.

Pet sins are another of life's vices that turn our hearts back to God in prayer. Of all my pet sins, and there are many, the most aggravating is the sin of discontent. The grass is always greener at the neighbors,' in a different apartment, or in a past life back in Florida. I am usually itching to move. I want to try something new, look at new surroundings, get to know different people . . . until an opportunity to move comes along. Then the Lord inevitably turns my heart back to Psalm 16: "LORD, you have assigned me my portion and my cup; you have made my lot secure. The boundary lines have fallen for me in pleasant places; surely I have a delightful inheritance" (verses 5,6). And a friend reminds me, "The Holy Spirit knows your address." I am fine for a while then.

Scripture abounds with prayers focusing our thoughts on specific requests. God's warehouse is never depleted, though it has been used (and neglected) for centuries. These written prayers in the Bible are recyclable; just try to wear them out.

You have given us the gift of words, dear Lord—words that meet in your will and our needs. I praise you for giving my heart the words to speak, even though you already know all its secrets. Amen.

*P*ray *continually.*

(1 Thessalonians 5:17)

CHAPTER SEVEN

Practice Prayer

My youngest brother, Pete, has a vivid imagination. We first noticed it when he was two. His favorite outfit was jeans and a white T-shirt with one of his rectangular-shaped blocks rolled up in the sleeve. With thumbs up, he answered us in a long, drawn-out monosyllable, "Aaaaaaaaaay!" He was our miniature Fonzie from the TV sitcom "Happy Days."

At four his imagination gravitated to imaginary friends. We would watch out the window as he and his "teammates" carried out play after play in a sweaty game of football. We would listen, amazed, when he would come into the kitchen, remove his helmet, and proceed to describe each play in detail. He always included the role that each of the others had carried out in each play. His face was red and dripping with perspiration. To him the game was real. He took his football and his imaginary friends very seriously. As well as entire seasons of football, Pete's vivid imagination provided him with harrowing motorcycle rides, death-defying feats of physical strength, and impossible odds against enemy warriors in battle.

When life doesn't seem to meet all our needs, we like to fill the gaps in our own creative ways, don't we? Some of these ways may be harmless, like imaginary friends. Others take us beyond the boundaries of those things that are God-pleasing. This is when we find ourselves caught in a web of self-destruction.

You can have regular communication with your loving God without using your imagination. When it comes to prayer, the image of an angel sitting on each person's shoulder is neither accurate nor helpful. Our mighty God is our constant companion, not in an imaginary way, but in a spiritual way. You may have to toss your own bales in the harvest, but he is right beside you in the process, providing strength for the task and safety around the machines.

God loves it when we wrestle with him in prayer. (Though it's Jacob who has the wrestling experience in Genesis chapter 32, it isn't only a "guy thing," ladies.) The beauty of being in God's presence is that he is not a figment of our imagination—he's real. Though not visible, he is physically present with us. We have Jesus' own promise regarding that. So we can take God along in every aspect of our day and have continual communication with him in prayer.

Nehemiah's example

A wonderful example from the Bible of someone who was constant in prayer is Nehemiah. Check your Bible's table of contents. He wrote his own book! The first few chapters are an easy read, and they give you an idea of what is contained in the rest of the book. A little bit of background is in order here: Nehemiah was a Jew serving the king of Persia. He was one of many who were taken prisoner in the destruction of Jerusalem. His position was one of official cupbearer, or wine taster. The purpose of another man tasting the king's wine was to spare the king from a potential assassination by poison. Nehemiah's situation alone made prayer a practical endeavor.

Jews from the middle and upper classes had been carried off into exile. Some families had been left behind in Jerusalem to farm the land. It was an embarrassment, however, for these people to remain living in the land of God's chosen people with destruction all around and no means or manpower to do the repairs. When Nehemiah received word of this state of affairs, he was understandably upset.

I like Nehemiah. He was an upbeat kind of guy, which can probably be attributed to his open connection with God. Nehemiah always seems to have had God at the forefront of his thoughts. For days he prayed about the conditions in Jerusalem, forming a plan in his mind with God's help. He prayed for success as he waited for an opportunity to present his plan. And when the king finally did agree to give Nehemiah an audience, Nehemiah prayed fervently before speaking.

The king granted Nehemiah permission to return to Jerusalem so that he could carry out his plan of restoring some semblance of order. But not everyone was pleased. Some even believed that Nehemiah's efforts to rebuild Jerusalem's wall bordered on the naïve; they had a good laugh over Nehemiah's proposal.

But Nehemiah never gave in to their mocking. Instead, he prayed. With complete confidence he even called down God's judgment on the scoffers.

God granted success, even as others continually sought to foil the project. Nehemiah reports, "We prayed to our God and posted a guard day and night to meet this threat. When our enemies heard that we were aware of their plot and that God had frustrated it, we all returned to the wall, each to his own work" (Nehemiah 4:9,15).

As the challenges continued and still others opposed the building of the wall, God gave Nehemiah strength. And the people gave credit where credit was due: "So the wall was completed . . . in fifty-two days. When all our enemies heard about this, all the surrounding nations were afraid and lost their self-confidence, because they realized that this work had been done with the help of our God" (Nehemiah 6:15,16).

The story, however, does not end there. Rebuilding the wall seemed a small detail in comparison to the rebuilding of God's people and the renewing of their focus on the Holy One of Israel. Nehemiah remained strong in faith and, with God's help, he appointed leaders in the church. Worship was restored according to God's plan. The people held a celebration when the wall was rededicated. And "the sound of rejoicing in Jerusalem could be heard far away" (Nehemiah 12:43).

Through prayer and perseverance Nehemiah continued his service to the Lord until the wall, the priesthood, and worship were restored. Still, with great humility he prayed, "Remember me for this also, O my God, and show mercy to me according to your great love" (Nehemiah 13:22). Nehemiah's joy is notable in both his trials and his successes. For it all he gave glory to God.

The same joy is ours. Using our gift of prayer consistently, we gain a great appreciation for it and find true enjoyment in its use.

Making prayer into a habit

Many times our connections with the Lord strengthen as we are humbled by heaven-sent tests. We are encouraged to make prayer a habit through these tests and through practice.

Everyday events, sights, and sounds are signals that move us to pray. Years ago, while traveling with a friend, I listened as she prayed for the victims of a car accident. Today, if I find myself crawling along at a snail's pace in traffic, I pray for those in vehicles around me—that God would give the drivers patience, calm cranky children, and call any unbelievers to faith in the Savior's name. I pray for whatever might be the cause of the delay. I pray for road construction workers who work in dangerous locations along highways. If I come across prison inmates on roadside crews, I pray for faith, repentance, and that they might find resolution to their lives of crime in order to live new lives.

Some children have greater behavior challenges than others. In the classroom that is no secret. Terry was one of those students. We were well into the third quarter when I noticed that Terry was acting out less and less. When I shared this good news with his mother, she told me that since the first day of the school year, the family had been praying in the car before Terry and his brother entered school in the morning. What a thrill to hear her give the glory to God for answered prayers!

On my morning walk I pray for the neighbors, especially those who have no knowledge of the Savior. I rejoice over those who have put their faith on display in lawn ornaments or signs and posters. I pray for repentance in those caught in sinful lifestyles. If I should hear angry words or children crying, I pray for an extra measure of love and patience in their relationships.

Guy Dowd, National Teacher of the Year in 1987, gave a glorious testimony to his faith in Christ and to how he was able to share that faith in classrooms where he taught. His habit was to sit in one student's desk each morning and pray for that boy or girl. As he shared that student's seat for a moment or two, he attempted to see life from his or her perspective.

Other prayer ideas

Don't we all hate to be put on hold when calling businesses and even friends? Don't let the "elevator music" lull you into a subconscious state of mind. Use these precious, God-given moments to pray for your friend, a business acquaintance, or the business at the other end of the line.

Maybe you've found yourself holding down a chair in a waiting room longer than you imagined. Turn your eyes outward to the needs of the other people sitting in the dentist office or doctor's waiting room. Offer words of prayer for the medical concerns of the people you see. Then share a warm smile to their worried eyes or words of encouragement to their anxious ears. Maybe God will call you to help an overwhelmed mother, comfort a grandma in pain, or read a story to a sleepy toddler who is up past the appointed nap time.

How about the person who has overlooked the "20 items or less" notice above the express lane in your favorite food market? Or when you're caught in the supermarket rush hour and it seems every other checkout clerk must have the day off? Pray for the person who didn't read the sign. (Maybe that person really can't read it.) Pray for the management, that they would be better able to organize work schedules. Pray for the baggers, that they might serve joyfully. Give thanks for those doing their best work in adverse conditions. Praise God for places where food is in abundance. Ask for his help to stretch your food dollar. Ask him to help you see ways in which you can share whatever you have with others.

It doesn't take many minutes of the evening news to discover some severe prayer needs. Need I say more?

Finally, as you get out of bed, give thanks that you have a place to lay your head. When you look in the mirror, ask God for forgiveness for your many shortcomings and for the grace to let his light shine in your life for others to see. If you don't already have enough visuals that will remind you to pray, list some reminders on post-it notes. Place them wherever they will be able to serve as reminders. If post-it notes aren't big enough, try index cards. Trade thoughts or lists with a friend or with other members of your Bible class. Turn in the lists and trade again. Share prayer ideas with friends. Pray that your eyes and minds be open to new prayer needs in your world.

My brother Pete is now Dad to two precious boys. The oldest has been blessed with the imagination of his father. Timothy creates situations in his mind throughout the day and shares them with whoever is available to listen. He too has found companionship in his imagination. Thankfully, Pete has also shared his God-given faith with his children and has brought them to the Savior through Baptism. He has given his children the best gift of all, a *real* ever-present companion, who even answers prayers.

*L*ord and Savior of all, be our constant companion and guide—a silent but active listener to every conversation. Use us as advocates for others through our prayers. Amen.

*T*he LORD brings death and makes alive; he brings down to the grave and raises up. The LORD sends poverty and wealth; he humbles and he exalts.

(1 Samuel 2:6)

CHAPTER EIGHT

Lipstick on the Wall

I lifted the lid of the washing machine and gasped. My load of whites was glowing with streaks of pink. The color was *flaming fuchsia*. I remember thinking my new shorts felt a little heavy when I dropped them in. But, of course, I was in too much of a hurry to check the pockets. Now my clothes will pay for my haste with another run through the cycle—this time with bleach.

When there are lipstick marks on my laundry, I've got no one to blame but myself. When there are lipstick marks on the wallpaper, your child genius probably discovered the code to the secret compartment of your purse. Maybe there's a magic formula for lipstick removal available at your local hardware store.

When it comes to prayer, I wish God would spell out his answers with my favorite shade of lipstick. How else am I to know God's *yeses* from his *nos* and *maybes*?

In teaching I use a visual that helps children remember that God's answers to our prayers come in a variety of shades and hues. I call it the "traffic light analogy." The traffic light analogy says that the green of the traffic light represents God's answer of yes. The red light means he's saying no to your request. Children have to be reminded, just as we do, that no is still an answer. Yellow reminds us we may have to wait patiently on God's holy wisdom; he sees a better time or a better way, or both. Most importantly, I teach the children that any God-given answer always has our best interests in mind.

I've already asked for signs while praying at a traffic light. When I open my eyes and the light is green, that means I will go buy that new car. If the light is yellow, I have to wait until the car dealer runs its July 4th sale. Red means I should wait until the car of my dreams comes out in, say . . . teal. If you're following my tactics, you can see that I never have to wait since the light is not going to turn from red to yellow. And, the way I plan it, God never really means no. But with that line of thinking, I figure he'll probably make me keep the heap I'm driving now until it dies.

Green light

Obviously, we want all of God's answers to be in the green light range. May we have a loan for a new house? Yes! Please let Nancy be good in school today. Yes! Lord, let all my lab tests come back negative. Yes! Praise to our wonderful God because his answers often are "yes."

Some friends of mine received word that there were complications in the development of their unborn child. They had prayed for a child and both were prepared to become the parents of a son with special needs. As they prepared, they prayed and asked many others to pray with them concerning his health and development. The first tests were not conclusive. God almighty can do anything. After two months of patiently praying, new tests came back: All appeared normal. Yes!

Are you ever surprised by God's green light answers? "Congratulations, you got your raise." I did? "You have a healthy baby girl." I do? "You just won the lottery!" You're kidding. Often when I look back at the lists of prayers in my journal, several have been given the green light that I didn't even remember praying about.

I know of a church where people are actually praying to win the lottery. They intend to pay off the building debt with the money. It's still a yellow light on that one, but you never know . . .

There are times when God's answer is quite clearly yes, but we may simply choose not to believe it. I remember some friends who wanted to move out of state to the city of their dreams. They had been praying about it for years. Then the husband's company announced a variety of transfer options. Their dream town was on the list. They continued in prayer. "Let's just see what the schools are like, in case we should move there." Their investigation found lovely Christian teachers in the local public schools. They continued to pray. "What's the real estate situation like?" "Oh, that reasonable?" "Let's put in an offer; who knows what'll happen?" Offer accepted. "Oh, but we'd still have to sell our house. The market in this neighborhood isn't that great right now." Their house sold the first week on the market. She applied for a job in her field. An interview was granted. Still, they asked me, "Do you think we're doing the right thing by moving?" To me, the lipstick was on the wall.

I've often thought skywriting would be a lovely way for God to communicate his answers to prayers. While relaxing on the beach in Florida, I would watch the planes dipping and swirling through the sky, wondering if there would ever be a message for me: "Take the call to Madison." "Buy the little blue house." "I love you, Jane." The closest it ever came was, "Sonny's Bistro Happy Hour: 6-10."

A yellow light

The *yellow* or *wait* answers from God are, for some people, the most frustrating. The unknown appears to leave the believer hanging. Coming out of college, my picture of life included teaching for two or three years, getting married, and having a family. I had not thought about it that much. It's the way life happens. For years I lived for what was surely "right around the corner."

On my 34th birthday, I got a message from a friend that changed my life. It said, "May this be the year God reveals his plan for your life." The proverbial two-by-four hit me from point-blank range. I had been teaching for 12 years. Twelve years. The realization came to me: *This is it*. This *is* God's plan for my life. And what's more, *I kind of like it*. Not every day, of course. But I'm not cleaning lipstick off my wallpaper either.

Hannah is a godly mentor. Her heavenly Father helped her to move on when she was dealing with a yellow-light answer to her prayer (1 Samuel chapter 1).

In Hannah's culture it was embarrassing to be infertile, as she was. In contrast, her husband's other consort was prolific in childbearing—and very verbal about it. This went on for years. Though her husband was loving and supportive, the fertile womb of the other wife was too irritating to bear. And Hannah's biological clock kept right on ticking.

Hannah prayed in the temple. She prayed with such agony of heart and soul, a priest observing her behavior believed she was intoxicated.

God gave Hannah peace of heart. We are told, "Then she went her way and ate something, and her face was no longer downcast" (1 Samuel 1:18).

Hannah finally gave her worry and frustration over to God, where they belonged. Could this be what God was waiting for her to do? "In the course of time Hannah conceived and gave birth to a son" (1 Samuel 1:20).

The scriptural account of Hannah's life does not tell us that she fervently prayed about her barrenness for years, although she certainly may have. Does God have a measuring cup of prayer, that, once filled, lets his answer come forth? What is the right number of times to pray for something: once, fifteen, or a lifetime? Why might one person's prayer be answered in one request while the rest of us feel as though we have been standing around waiting for a long time?

There are many reasons why God might have us wait for his answers to our prayers. God's answers often appear when we become what he wants us to become and when we see what he wants us to see. It's called growth! Growth may involve greater trust, vision, insight, wisdom, or love. He may be looking for faithfulness, honesty, dedication, or conviction. He does not count prayers, he measures faith. He does not compare one person's faith with that of another, but measures personal growth. If you've matured lately, treat yourself to a new shade of lipstick, deeper and bolder, please.

There's one more aspect of Hannah's situation that screams for discussion. Hannah made a vow to God. She promised to return the child to him if he gave her one. Did Hannah's bargain with God have anything to do with his answer? Can God be bought with sacrifice?

Living on the western plains of our country is a godly wife and mother of two. When this mother was born, she had a hole in her heart. At the time of the surgery to repair the hole, she was three years old. Her parents prayed for success. They vowed that, should God see fit to bring their daughter through surgery, they would give her over to him as a teacher in his church.

The surgery was a success and Corrine grew strong and healthy. God had answered her parents' prayers before they had vowed to give their daughter as a teacher. Their further reward: their daughter always knew she was going to be a teacher. It became her heart's desire to want nothing *but* to become a teacher. No career was forced upon her. No square peg made to fit a round hole. God accepted their sacrifice. And their compensation was joy untold.

God also answered Hannah's prayer without first seeing the sacrifice on her part. She was given the son her longing heart desired without any further action on her part . . . no strings attached. Her promise to God had been to give her son over to the work of the Lord. She kept her promise out of love and thanksgiving to the Lord by giving Samuel over to work in the temple.

There was further reward, given without request on Hannah's part. God not only blessed her with one son, but several children. We learn a little later on in the story that "the LORD was gracious to Hannah; she conceived and gave birth to three sons and two daughters" (1 Samuel 2:21).

Vows and sacrifices, such as those just described, are gifts of love from God's children to their loving heavenly Father. God is honored by them, pleased with them, glorified in these actions. They are yet another avenue for praising, exalting, and magnifying our gracious God. Thankfulness for what God has done, also a gift from him, motivates us to follow through on a vow. God in his wisdom already knows at the time of the promise whether faithfulness abounds. He cannot be bribed or bought, only loved and sought. He loves and gives from the same gracious heart that gave his only Son. We cannot know the blessings in store for the faithful.

God has a plan. The light may be yellow for the prayer you feel God has not yet answered. But don't let the waiting slow you down. Life goes on. That is, keep doing what you're doing. Do it well. Put one foot in front of the other and move on with joy and energy.

The Israelites kept moving through the desert, though they had no idea where God would take them. They had a cloud to follow by day and a tower of fire to follow when it was dark (Exodus 13:21,22). We don't have a cloud or pillar of fire to follow, but our job is to keep our eyes on the cross of Jesus, in light and in dark times. Leave it to the Holy Spirit to keep our feet on the right path.

Red light

There are times we all see red. God's answers to some prayers are bound to be no. Some we should not be too surprised about: no, you may not make your first million by age 25. No, you may not make it through raising two teenagers unscathed by frustration. And no, dinner is not going to appear on the table every night at 6:00 . . . at least not without tipping for delivery.

Denied prayers may come with great disappointment. The loan fell through for the purchase of your dream home, even though everything felt so right each step of the way. Your husband filed for divorce just when you believed the knots in your life together were untangling. Your application for the adoption of your first child was set aside in favor of another family. The depths of heartache felt from God's red lights are more often than not painful beyond all measure.

Does a red light answer mean you are lacking in faith? Is God viewing your faith life as inferior? He may be challenging you to grow in other ways, serve in other avenues, and is definitely teaching you to trust his wisdom in all things. Keep an open mind to all the possibilities and options in life. Our loving Lord wants the best for all believers. He doesn't promise every earthly dream fulfilled. (Then earth would be heaven.) And for good reason. He still has work to do, in us and through us.

Christian sisters, we dare never lose hope. For us to despair is to deny the effectiveness of Christ on the cross. He died that we might live, and he didn't mean just survive.

> Thanks be to God! He gives us the victory through our Lord Jesus Christ. Therefore, my dear brothers (sisters), stand firm. Let nothing move you. Always give yourselves fully to the work of the Lord, because you know that your labor in the Lord is not in vain. (1 Corinthians 15:57,58)

No matter how God answers your prayers, put some lipstick on those lips where it belongs and smile! God listens. He hears. He knows you. He knows your needs. And he is smiling down upon you in shades of greens, yellows, and reds.

Lord Jesus Christ, you were sacrificed so I might live victoriously. Teach me to pray with confidence, live life boldly, and trust in God's answers to my prayers. Amen.

The eyes of the L ORD are on the righteous
and his ears are attentive to their cry.

(Psalm 34:15)

CHAPTER NINE

Join the Chorus

I love to sing. Although I'm not sure everyone under the sun loves hearing me sing. History shows that my vocal presentations have not been greeted with invitations for encores. I solo mainly in the classroom. The kids don't complain.

I especially enjoy singing when I'm by myself. Every note doesn't have to be perfect when there is an audience of one. If I sing along with the radio or a CD and I forget a word, the original artist fills it in and does a much better job.

Singing in the car is harmless. I've seen people at intersections in the act, jaw dropped, head back, eyes closed, vocalizing at the top of their voices. I try to avoid that pose if at all possible.

Is the shower performance a guy thing? The vote is still out on that one. Ladies, if all you shower soloists would drop me a line, I'll add the information to my statistics and get back to you.

I also enjoy singing with a crowd. With others singing around me, I sing out much more confidently. I know the others will cover for me and vice versa.

To join or not to join

Do you pray solo or in chorus? Personal prayer happens any time, any place. Brief clips of prayer-songs burst forth at a child's home run or a narrowly missed accident. Long, strenuous arias of heart-wrenching prayers pour out in a hospital waiting room. Sweet melodies are whispered during times of meditation.

Thankfully, being a prayer soloist does not require the knowledge of any kind of actual musical theory. You need not read notes, count time, or hold notes until you're blue.

Solo prayers are most comfortable for many Christians because, first of all, no one cares what you look like at the time. You can be crumpled from sleep, sweaty from a work-out, or grubby from the garden. If you turn the words around, it doesn't confuse anyone else. The Holy Spirit is well ahead of us in technology and provides enhancing background vocals. He even "cleans up" the final take, tuning and polishing unfinished prayer thoughts.

If you write down your prayers, you've got a soundtrack to sing along with next time. And you are guaranteed an audience with the One who encourages repeat performances. Daily.

Several heroes of faith went solo on prayer tours. Abraham was the Pavarotti of prayer when he alone prayed for Sodom and Gomorrah (Genesis chapter 18). Moses, one of the most unlikely and unwilling of prayer soloists, often took center stage in prayer. Occasionally the Israelites sang back-up or came in on a chorus, but they were not always dependable. Elijah and Jonah both prayed mournful dirges as they neared the end of their lives. The common thread in all their prayers was the audience. Though they often prayed unaccompanied by another human voice, our mighty God was listening to every phrase, every cadence and crescendo of the voice, every melodic measure of the heart. The angel told Zechariah, "Do not be afraid, Zechariah; your prayer has been heard" (Luke 1:13). Put your own name into this verse. You can be sure that it is true.

But solo is not the only way to go. Two or three or more gathered in God's name often pray when together. The voice combinations are diverse. Your ladies' group is a treble choir of voices. They join together in prayer-songs most often about friendships, marriage, children, the home, and dreams of the heart. The repertoire is certainly not limited to these selections, however. They may also offer musical works concerning missions, outreach, world peace, and turmoil in the family.

A unique and lovely sound is heard in the family prayer chorus. Sizes of family ensembles vary from the duet of a husband and wife to the trio, quartet, quintet, and so on.

The most common unison prayer of the family is heard at the dinner table. Memorized prayers are often spoken together in thanks and praise for meals. These dinnertime prayers are incredibly valuable in bringing words of appreciation to God. However, diverting from the chorus to solo verses of individual family members is also important. As parents lead the prayers, they are setting examples for their children in praying personally. They are also providing models for their children on how to someday lead their own families in prayer. As you can see, the family prayer chorus has a way of echoing on and on, long after the family circle is dispersed and into the autumn of its life.

You may be so blessed as to belong to an ensemble of coworkers that prays together. Many groups of pastors and teachers enjoy this privilege. Their voices, joined in prayer-song, are able to bring ministry needs before the Lord with the distinctive support of all those present.

One church I belonged to had a men's choir appropriately named "Hymns of Praise." These *hims* raised songs of prayer and praise with their male voices. Other groups of men in prayer may be a church's council and voters. There are also some men's prayer groups that meet for breakfast or lunch at a restaurant or in someone's home. Imagine the strength in the prayers of those mighty soldiers of faith.

Prayer-groups for children include Sunday schools or classroom prayer-choirs. Young hearts and voices are also united in prayer at Pioneer meetings or at other church children's club meetings. Some churches even have a children's evangelism team that prays regularly for the lost. What power in those prayers!

Aside from the typical church choir, your congregation in its worship services becomes a prayer-choir. Voices unite week after week in the familiar prayer to our heavenly Father.

Other selections include prayers such as Luther's morning or evening prayers or responsive prayers in which the congregation responds to the worship leader. Many hymns and songs are also prayers.

Praying together

If the prayer of a single voice is clearly heard and understood by our mighty God, then what can be the value of voices united in prayer? Whether in personal prayer or group prayer, remember that prayer first of all changes us, the pray-ers. Praises, problems, and possibilities are released to God's control and exchanged for his peace. Praying together in groups encourages us. Just knowing that others are praying the same request helps us know that the prayer is within God's will.

Unison praying, or group prayer, where one prays while others listen, is often called "agreeing in prayer." This simply means that all people present are of the same mind concerning the request. "Yes, we all would like the Johnsons' baby to be healthy." "Yes, we all want to get home safely in the storm." "You bet we'd like to increase the kingdom of believers." Sometimes that assent is verbalized: while another person is praying, the rest of the members of the group utter "amen" in agreement.

Agreement in prayer adds volume to our requests. But not volume measured in decibels. We do not need volume as if we need to awaken a sleeping deity. Our omniscient God is constantly aware of our needs and stands ready to hear any and all prayers. A word of caution is appropriate here. While prayer truly is a fruit of our faith, it is not a work that will in any way benefit our salvation. God does not give bonus points or special encores to those who pray in groups. He does not move anyone closer to the gate of heaven for service spent in prayer. He will not answer prayer requests based on the length of time spent in group prayer or based on the number of people praying together in a certain group. The only basis by which God answers prayer is the work done for us by his Son, Jesus. Be careful that the work-righteous kind of thinking does not slip into your understanding of prayer. It is an easy mistake for sinful humans to make since we are always interested in replacing the true God with a god that looks more like us. The human inclination says, "I don't need God; *I* can do this for myself." And before you know it, prayer mistakenly becomes our own idea of how to get to heaven.

The early Christian church was characterized by its constant prayer in groups. This trend began immediately after Jesus had left his disciples by ascending into heaven. What his disciples did provides a beautiful insight into how Jesus wants all of his followers to view this wonderful gift of prayer. We read:

> Then they returned to Jerusalem from the hill called the Mount of Olives, a Sabbath day's walk from the city. When they arrived, they went upstairs to the room where they were staying. Those present were Peter, John, James and Andrew; Philip and Thomas, Bartholomew and Matthew; James son of Alphaeus and Simon the Zealot, and Judas son of James. They all joined together constantly in prayer, along with the women and Mary the mother of Jesus, and with his brothers. (Acts 1:12-14)

The disciples' example was followed by the many new converts who were added to the numbers of the church. When Peter and John suffered persecution from the Jewish High Council for preaching about Christ's crucifixion and resurrection, the group joined together in prayer. "When they heard this, they raised their voices together in prayer to God. . . . After they prayed, the place where they were meeting was shaken. And they were all filled with the Holy Spirit and spoke the word of God boldly" (Acts 4:24,31).

Do you remember the fairy tale in which all the animals are trapped by a fox within a home around a dinner table? In a quick-thinking request, the animals ask if they might pray before the meal begins—a meal in which they are to be the main course. One animal begins to pray, then another joins in until all are praying and praying and praying at great length.

Their hope is that the predatory fox will eventually lose interest and depart in peace.

One possible lesson of this fairy tale is that if we be so continually in prayer, our enemy, the devil, may lay aside his intent to destroy our faith and give up. (It's an interesting concept, but one that also leans in the direction of the do-it-yourself theology on how to get to heaven.)

Jesus has already completed the work of defeating the devil. There is an echo to the phrase *it is finished* that says of Satan, "*He* is finished." In the final judgment, the divine Judge will bind Satan in the chains of eternity. Our prayers will have had nothing to do with that cosmic event. It was laid out in God's holy plan before the beginning of time. But that doesn't mean we can't or shouldn't pray for such an end. Remember, in prayer our will lines up with God's will.

A contemporary composer of choral music gives this advice to his church choir, "Keep your eyes on the director and your mind on the Savior." In a prayer chorus, both positions are one and the same person—Jesus.

*P*raise to you, Lord Jesus, because you direct our prayers to the Father's heavenly throne whether they are the expressions of one voice or many. Amen.

We constantly pray for you . . .

(2 Thessalonians 1:11)

CHAPTER TEN

Prayers of Women at Work

"I am woman, hear me roar." These song lyrics from a few decades back emphasize the power of women and their ability to speak on issues and make themselves heard. The implication is that the female of our species has the capability of accomplishing much more than anyone previously thought possible.

Visualize women roaring. In your mind, if you are roaring, are you having a good day or a bad day? I tend to do the roaring lion routine when kids get out of control or when the house hasn't been swept in a month or when, in the first minute of a precious hour to myself, the phone rings.

These days women seem to wear many more hats than in previous generations. I have a friend who rewired her fixer-upper of a house. She installed her own toilet and built the deck around the family pool along with a hardwood swing for the backyard. She's a living, breathing, tool-belt bearing, do-it-yourself queen—a roaring lion with power tools. Christian mother that she is, she also has a brace of tools that you won't find hanging from a tool belt. She lives her prayer life in a way that boldly proclaims the power that is at her disposal through prayer. Her faith life is proof that women can get to work without wielding steel.

Our spiritual lives, roaring with concerns, can be powerfully active in the area of prayer. We can be consumed with the tall task of constructing spiritual and emotional support systems with others as we call on our heavenly Father in prayer.

Praying for others

A concerned mother is puzzled about her teenager's unusual behavior. I'll pray for her. Your friend's husband is under tremendous stress over a special project at work. I'll pray for him. Your elderly parents can no longer live alone, but what can you do when you are 500 miles away? Someone says, "I'll pray for you." Those words may occasionally be uttered in a help-less, I-don't-know-what-else-to-say frame of mind. But they should not become empty promises.

Even after we are made aware of a situation, we don't always know the details. You may not know the struggling person very well. You may not have been aware that a person discussed in an evangelical conversation is in need of prayer. Being the per-sonal thing that prayer is, you might reason that someone could feel you are interfering by offering to pray. Don't be deterred. Prayer is one of the few things in life that no one on earth can stop you from doing. Satan would love to tear down your resolve and conviction to pray by making you believe that prayer is banned in those cases in which your loving compas-sion is not welcomed. Jesus said just the opposite. He said that we are to pray even for our enemies—the people who despise us, for whatever reason.

Most of the real enemies that I have probably don't really care to have me praying for them. But that has not yet stopped me from exercising my right to pray, my privilege to pray. My prayers for them are the only ways in which I can show my love for them.

Scripture reports more than one case of believers praying in prison—in the very presence of their enemies. Who was to stop them?

When Daniel was discovered praying in the privacy of his room, in spite of the king's decree outlawing such prayer activ-ity, he was arrested and thrown into a den of lions. You know the rest of the story.

Use what information you have and get to work. Rarely will someone feel you have overstepped your boundaries.

Next, as opportunities arise and you discover that you are so gifted, pray with others on location. Put yourself in their work boots. An offer to pray with someone in need can be a genuine comfort. Invite them to pray for you, as well. These wonderful relationships that are built on Christ are always a two-way thoroughfare. You too will be encouraged to receive God's gift of peace while someone prays with you.

Sometimes it's a good idea to pray about your prayer life first. Pray for a mind turned toward continual prayer. Pray for a heart of love for others. Pray that God might give you an understanding of a situation, along with the words that express your sanctified desires. Ask God for renewed strength to continue in prayer until his answers are evident. Ask him to extend the measure of your patience so that it will coincide with his timing. You are going to approach heaven's throne with some passionate feelings about the mountains you want to move. Ask him to help you understand and accept the fact that he has given you those mountains to scale as an exercise of faith.

What to pray

Now that you are armed and dangerous—to the devil, that is—what ought we as women pray for when others are in need? Obviously, some situations present themselves as urgent. The salvation of lost souls, for example. Serious illnesses or injuries that are life-threatening call for some urgent prayers. These are special moments in which people are often more open to the vital story that Scripture has to tell. "Does your Uncle Charlie know Jesus as his Savior?" If not, you will know what to pray for. But don't forget to include in your prayer people who are closely connected to the circumstances: family, friends, children, and neighbors. They may also be in need of your prayers as they reach out to Uncle Charlie with the message of the gospel, his only hope. Pray that hearts become open to receiving the gift of the Holy Spirit. For the believers, pray for strength of faith, peace of mind and heart, and an extra measure of courage to stand in the face of every challenge. Ask that God's will be done, then pray that whatever his will might be, it may be received with thankful hearts.

Some situations will probably require long-term prayer. Keep these situations on your prayer list. Pray regularly for your church family, your children, and your children's friends. Pray for your children's school and schools in general. Our government and its leaders desperately need our prayers, particularly in the wake of national tragedies and formidable enemies of our nation's security. But the most difficult item on your prayer list will be your personal enemies. Make a special effort to always pray for those who hate you or the things you stand for. And begin that prayer by asking God to first help you to genuinely love them.

Who needs my prayers?

The list of people for whom we might pray is really quite endless. You can pray regularly for those in your church's fellowship of believers and for those Christians who are not from your fellowship. Pray for those who sit near you in a worship service and for those who worship in Jesus' name in faraway places. Offer prayers for the members of a committee on which you serve. Your pastors, vicar, principal, teachers, and secretaries all need regular prayers from the people they serve. Ask God to help them remain faithful to his Word and to preach, teach, and live fearlessly in obedience to his will. Pray for their families who support them in their work.

Children need the prayers of adults. Moms, with the hearts of love you have for your own, this may be the longest part of your prayer list. You want their faith to last a lifetime so you pray for them to stay strong in the truth of Scripture. You want them to learn to pray. You want them to be a friend to others. You want them to have health, wisdom, energy, and gifts to serve. You want them to abstain from sexual relations until marriage, to have a godly spouse, or to have the strength and vision to remain in a single life.

Our schools need every prayer we can offer. Guns, sexual misconduct from a few bad-apple teachers, budgetary constraints, disrespect for authority, promiscuity, and drugs all threaten to drag education under in one way or another. Children need love and respect demonstrated to them daily. Ask that God provide for their safety. Ask him to provide strength and patience for every teacher and solid leadership in the ranks. And if your children have experienced the blessing of being able to attend a Christian school, thank God daily for the availability of Christian education. Ask him to make sure that the truth of his Word is taught clearly. Pray that an atmosphere of love will always permeate your child's school and that the love of Jesus will be demonstrated daily in prayer. And, while you are at it, pray that this same love will be shown by all the members of the staff for one another.

Why not form a prayer group that prays for your children and their school? Ours is called *Moms in Touch*. They meet once a week over a noon hour. They share Scripture verses and insights regarding faith and children. They pray for each teacher, each special need, and each event as it approaches on the school calendar. They especially pray that Christ will remain the clear and apparent focus of every school event. After these moms began praying together, several changes in attitudes among both teachers and students were noticed during the school year.

Where can we start when praying for our government leaders and the laws of our land? At home, perhaps: your town mayor, your state's governor, all the people who work to govern, judges, legislators, district attorneys, law enforcement, security people. Then broaden the scope and don't stop until you've included our nation's president in your prayer thoughts. Do not hesitate to ask God to infuse the power of his saving Word in the lives of these people. Your leaders need your prayers for their physical, emotional, and spiritual strength.

In the classroom I have students write letters to the current president on his birthday or when we study the unit on Washington, DC. They are very bold in the questions they ask. Many of them tell the president that they are praying for him. Demonstrating your respect for government leaders sets an example for your children. Begin with prayer.

Women of the Word, we have a God-given voice in our soul, and he hears us whether we roar or whisper. Satan may prowl about roaring his lies, but when God's women roar, he's caged by the power of our God.

Make me strong in my life of prayer, dear Lord, that all the enemies of my soul will fall, and I will live triumphantly in your strength and power. Amen.

I urge, then, first of all, that requests, prayers, intercession and thanksgiving be made for everyone. (1 Timothy 2:1)

CHAPTER ELEVEN

Prayer Supports

Check out the catalogs, friends. Any quality collection of women's garments includes several items designed to help us hold it all together. The lovely thing about modern technology is that these support items are now so cleverly disguised. Under wires hidden in seams, strategically placed panels or pads, control top hose or total support hose. We can now have help holding our shoulders back, stomach in, and glutes tight. Then there are the skin toners that can make us look ten years younger. Unfortunately, it's all quite temporary.

There are oh-so-many areas of life where we seek help to hold it all together—little gimmicks and gadgets to help us cover all the bases. Why not seek the same for our prayer life, as well? If prayer is important, and we know it is, then let's organize ourselves to improve production. With support we can help one another keep prayer in its place of priority.

Keep a list

Women are already the queens of list-makers, so why not make some prayer lists?

I began keeping prayer lists years ago. I was already journaling, and adding lists of things to pray about became a natural part of that writing. I began with a spiral bound notebook. Later, I discovered the joy of writing in blank books. I pick them up whenever I see them on sale, the prettier the better, and I keep them with me as I go through my daily routines.

There are books available specifically designed for prayer journaling. Room is provided to write the date, your prayer, and to note God's unique answer to that prayer. These books make excellent gifts.

Our women's Bible study group keeps a prayer journal. When we arrive, a journal and a pen are available for us to begin writing our prayer requests. We leave the right side pages blank for listing answers. Before recording new prayers, we glance back over our lists and make notes in the book regarding any answers God has provided. However God decides to answer our prayers, we always rejoice in his perfect will. One woman wrote during the time of her dad's struggle with his health, "Keep my father's faith strong and ease his pain. Take him home peacefully when it's time." The entry of about six weeks later is a testimony to her faith and God's grace: "Dad left peacefully for his eternal home. Mom was by his side. No more suffering, pain, hospitals, nursing home. It was time." Praise God for his wisdom.

A slightly different twist to group-journaling is to have each woman bring her own personal journal. Thoughts and prayers can be written down during the study that can then be included in personal prayer time at home during the week.

There are some other kinds of prayer lists that are ready-made. If your church provides a directory of members, have a copy handy during your quiet time. You may want to decide just how many people you will pray for each day. Pick a number, such as five or ten. Mark your list and continue there the next time. When you come to the end of the roster, start over. Don't forget to keep your ears open when members speak of blessings evident in their lives. You don't even have to tell them that they have a "prayer angel" if you don't want to. Just glorify God in your heart and keep praying!

If your church has a Christian school, the school office staff may publish a roster of students. Use the roster of school families in the same way as was suggested above for the list of church members. Again, keep your ears open as parents chat after school or at school or church events. Make mental notes of areas where particular families might need prayers. Then listen for indications of the blessings that follow.

Another ready-made list is your family tree. Very few families have a professional version of their family tree, but you can sketch your own. Start with the oldest living relatives on the trunk. Add branches and limbs according to your understanding of your family's history. For one of my friends, using her family tree as a ready prayer list brought her Uncle Frank to mind. Uncle Frank still had no knowledge of his salvation in Christ Jesus. Though he lived across the country, my friend was able to locate a church a few blocks from his house. She called the church's pastor and explained her uncle's failing physical health and lack of spiritual health. The pastor visited her uncle and shared God's free gift of salvation with him. Her uncle responded with appreciation and joy, so thankful that someone cared enough to tell him of his Savior's love and grateful to learn that heaven was waiting for him.

Your neighborhood is another good place to begin formulating a prayer list. The rows of houses provide a natural list of families, large or small, to keep in your prayers. One man in California decided to pray a "five-a-day" plan for spiritual health. He prayed five blessings on five neighbors for five minutes a day for five days a week for five weeks. He marveled over the changes in his neighbors. They didn't clean up their yards and thus keep the peace. But to his surprise some did ask him what they could do to have the same life of peace and joy that he experienced through Christ.

The five-finger prayer is also a creative, "hands-on" prayer list. (No pun intended.) Starting with your shortest finger, your pinky, you are reminded to pray for the small people in life: children, nieces and nephews, children's friends, and their classmates at school. The next finger is typically the weakest finger. We are reminded to pray for those who are frail and infirm, the elderly, and those who are sick. The tallest finger reminds us to pray for those in positions of authority: pastors, teachers, group leaders, government leaders. The pointer indicates those near you: your family, relatives, and friends. Last, when extended, the thumb points your way. You may now pray for your own wants and needs.

Prayer circles

Praying with others is a helpful way to remain committed to your prayer life. Plan with a fellow Christian to pray together over breakfast at McDonald's, while your kids watch a movie, over the phone, or during a walk. Talk through your routines and look for a regular time to meet. You may feel awkward at first, but as you exercise your gift of prayer, your hearts will become comfortable with each other's thoughts. And the blessings will become self-evident.

You may want to try an informal women's prayer breakfast. Our group gathered twice a month on Saturday mornings. Between 8 and 12 of us took turns inviting the other women to our homes. The hostess would pre-select a short section of Scripture to share. Then she would begin the circle prayer. Each person would end her thoughts with the words, "Lord, hear our prayer." Then the turn would pass to the next. Some women read prayers from a favorite book. Others brought their lists. Some prayed their own thoughts as they came. We closed with thanks for our food and then enjoyed a lovely breakfast and fellowship.

Written prayers

In addition to the Lord's Prayer, many other valued and time-tested prayers have been written down for our continued use. Lutherans over the ages have found value in the use of Martin Luther's Morning and Evening Prayers. Devotional books often contain prayers for the day or season. Prayer books are valuable in keeping concerns before our minds and hearts that may not have otherwise presented themselves.

Table prayers are commonly remembered and repeated. Remember, though, oft-repeated prayers can become mindless muttering. Balance your prayer life with familiar prayers, written prayers, and those consisting of your own thoughts. Your own prayers may be written down and prayed again and again.

You may have other valuable methods to organize and maintain your prayer life. Share your ideas with others and add to the catalog of prayer-support ideas.

Lord, encourage me to continue to grow in my prayer life. Provide as much support as I need to help me maintain my connection to you in prayer. Amen.

*J*oin with others in following my example, brothers (sisters), and take note of those who live according to the pattern we gave you.

(Philippians 3:17)

CHAPTER TWELVE

Copy? Right!

Life on the west coast of Florida is made complete with an annual pass to Busch Gardens in Tampa. Animals graze on the plains of a park that resembles the Serengeti. Virtual-reality rides, bumper cars, and 55-miles-per-hour roller coasters thrill—or terrify—tourists. Music, dance, and stunt shows from around the world entertain and impress.

Most visitors agree that, besides the roller coasters, the sea lion show is their favorite attraction. The sea lions are occasionally joined in the comedy act by an odd otter and a homely walrus. Baited with buckets of raw fish, the crazy antics of these silly sea creatures leave their audiences rolling in the aisles. Of course, they have no idea how funny they are; they are merely responding to the rewards offered by the trainers—a mouthful of herring and a pat on the head.

Just as entertainment does not come naturally to a sea lion, serving God does not come naturally to sinful human beings. This is also true with regard to prayer. As we have already seen, God thankfully provides a good measure of instructional help to aid us in developing our prayer skills. And, in addition to his own model prayer, we have a perfect model of prayer-life application as we examine the ways in which Jesus used prayer during his stay on earth.

Following Christ's example

A prayer lifestyle is more caught than taught. By that I mean that we learn to pray best by following good examples, rather than from reading about prayer in books or listening to sermons about prayer. And there is no better example than Jesus himself. Like his disciples of two thousand years ago, we must, in faith, ask, "Lord, teach us to pray."

Christ taught prayer. His actions spoke volumes. He went off by himself to pray. He led others in prayer. He prayed among others, as at the raising of Lazarus. Consider what the Bible tells about that startling event:

> Then Jesus looked up and said, "Father, I thank you that you have heard me. I knew that you always hear me, but I said this for the benefit of the people standing here, that they may believe that you sent me." (John 11:41,42)

Jesus wanted the people standing around Lazarus' grave to know that he prayed, and that, through prayer, he had the power to raise the dead.

Of course, Jesus is God's Son. He could have raised Lazarus' lifeless body without uttering this public prayer. But for the benefit of others, he demonstrated his oneness with his Father by praying to him.

Prayer mentors

God's plan for the family would have a child's models be his or her parents. Pray with your children in the morning before school or work. Send them e-mail prayers. Include special prayer requests at mealtime. Pray as a family, gathered in the living room or at a child's bedside.

A child's baptismal sponsors have the God-given responsibility to pray for the special child they serve. A sponsor can become a fine model of prayer life to a child. Extended family members such as grandparents, aunts and uncles, cousins, and siblings can also be excellent models in sharing the routines of their prayer lives.

Pastors, vicars, Sunday school teachers, children's club leaders at church, and choir directors all have opportunities to lead young children in prayer and thereby set examples for them. It has been my practice for many years to pray unwritten, unmemorized prayers with children of all ages. I also allow them to pray with me. I usually learn as much from these sessions as the children. Children's prayers are so uninhibited! We share God's answers to our prayers. We call these our "praise reports." And we all cheer in thanks for what God has done. How my heart thrills when the children do not hesitate to pray for me and for one another.

At the beginning of a new school year, I take my journal to school. I tell the children in my classroom how I use my journal. I also tell them that my way is not the only way to keep a prayer journal going. I read short sections of my journal to them. And I share answers I have seen. I tell them about the prayers I have been praying and about those prayers for which I am awaiting an answer. Then I give the children an opportunity to write in their own journals. They open up their hearts in their prayers and record appropriate and meaningful Scriptures. Here is a sample entry from a third grader's journal: "'Give thanks to the LORD, call on his name; make known among the nations what he has done' (Psalm 105:1). Dear God, thank you for our food, thank you for a house, and thank you for Pastor Sims and Mrs. Sims. Thank you for giving me a faithful heart, and for a Savior who died on the cross. 'I will praise you forever for what you have done; in your name I will hope, for your name is good' (Psalm 52:9)."

Adults who are comfortable praying together create an atmosphere where other adults and children are comfortable praying aloud and freely with one another. Even if praying aloud in the presence of others is not at first easy, it becomes easier with practice. Your voice may shake. God doesn't mind. You may stumble over the words. So what? Do you always talk smoothly when you're having a conversation with your closest friends? You may forget a thought. Who's counting? God heard it even if you did not remember to say it out loud. Prayer is not a performance; it is a conversation. Bottom line: Just do it! God is waiting to bless you through your prayers.

No one is ever too old to learn to lead in prayer either. At a recent women's breakfast I asked if anyone would mind if we went around the table and each took a turn to pray. Heartfelt prayers were spoken. When the breakfast was over, one woman over 60 told me she had never prayed with a group before. She has been a willing participant several times since.

Contrary to a popular notion, pastors do not have a direct line to God that is in any way different from the prayer lines of other Christians. (Jesus is the royal High Priest for all of us. He is the only One who does our interceding for us, pastors cannot.) But pastors often have more experience at leading in prayer. The only way to get such experience is to practice!

The women's avenue for gaining experience is to look for opportunities to lead in prayer. Lead the women of the ladies' guild, a small group Bible study, or a mission society. Be a mentor to children and teenagers. Help others to see the blessings and benefits that come from an active prayer life. Follow the example of another or do it with your own style. No matter how you approach the task, take a leap of faith and lead. Others will benefit from your direction.

Constructing a prayer for a group setting

When it comes to prayer, some simple outlines that seem to work for everyone are available. Here's one that never fails to make good sense because it follows such a practical order. First, express repentance of sins for yourself or the group, if you are leading. Second, though I doubt anyone needs this reminder, include requests. Petition God for every sort of physical, spiritual, or emotional need. Third, thank God. Even if life has been the pits and you don't see a long list of things to be thankful for, you always have a Savior for which you are eternally grateful. Last, don't forget the praise!

It seems to me that we could use the most practice in the area of giving praise to God in our prayers. Take out a pencil and paper and list all the words you currently use to praise God. Go ahead, I'll wait. Still thinking? Not an easy task. This last school year my class and I made a concentrated effort to work on that very skill. Here are some of the examples we came up with. *I love you, Lord. You are a great God. Jesus, you are an awesome Savior. I praise you, Lord, for all you have done for me. You are the best, God.* We decided that everyone would try to remember to add a word or two of praise to every prayer. When everyone was accountable to the class (including me), our prayers blossomed with expressions of praise. The effect in our lives was that all of us were even more keenly aware of all that God has done for us and more focused on his role in our lives.

One Tuesday afternoon our classroom volunteer was an older woman from the congregation. She sat in the back and waited while a third grader read the devotion and began to lead the classroom prayer. Though we typically had only one row of students pray each day, this particular day they had decided they all wanted a turn. Each of the 16 children prayed. One after another. A broad range of prayers covering repentance, petitions, thanks, and praise winged heavenward. When they had finished, the woman exclaimed in amazement, "What are you raising here, a bunch of pastors and teachers?" I answered, "No, just Christians! You know, the priesthood of *all* believers." My heart swelled with pride, and I went straight to the bank with that fat herring.

Perhaps the best part of the sea lion show at Busch Gardens is the pre-show entertainment. A mime with a white-painted face, a colorful striped shirt, white gloves, and a silent nature imitates the visitors as they enter the stadium. It is typical for the mime to pick out any distinguishing feature and exaggerate it behind the guest's back. Man, woman, or child, the guests file in, searching for the perfect seat, oblivious to the copycat behind them.

In Christian life, we are the mimes, silently imitating the Christian behaviors of those who have had the benefit of previous experience before us. Other times we are the model, oblivious to those who may be copying us. In either role, may

God grant us the courage to live and lead for Christ, creating legacies of prayer and lives of service worthy of imitation.

Now to him who is able to do immeasurably more than all we ask or imagine, according to his power that is at work within us, to him be glory in the church and in Christ Jesus throughout all generations, for ever and ever! Amen. (Ephesians 3:20,21)